ANIMAL HUSBANDRY

Animal Husbandry

Stories of Relinquishment

EMILY HIPCHEN

Cover art design by Jacob Arms

Published by Serving House Books
Editor in Chief, William K. Lawrence
Lawrence Landing Company
Raleigh, North Carolina 27609

www.servinghousebooks.com

Serving House Books is a proud member of:

Independent Book Publishers Association
 and
Community of Literary Magazines and Presses

SERVING HOUSE BOOKS

For Mary Beth Govern
who was born in early 1964
and who died that November.

She was a testament.

Acknowledgements

Thank you to my friends who helped edit this manuscript, including Ralph Savarese and Elizabeth Boleman-Herring, and to my colleagues and friends who supported this writing, including Amy Cuomo, Marina Fedosik, Austin Jackson, Kate Peterson, Kendall Pope, Sayres Rudy, Grace Talusan, and Rachel Williams. I appreciate the support of Brown University and my colleagues in the English Department and the Nonfiction Writing Program, especially Rick Rambuss, Jonathan Readey, and Ravit Reichman. Versions of some of these chapters appeared separately in the following publications:

"A Remembrance of Things Past Remembering." *Weekly Hubris*, 30 Nov. 2022, weeklyhubris.com/remembrance-of-things-past-remembering/.

"Broody." *Bayou Magazine*, vol. 59, 2013, pp. 68–74.

"Ducking." *Bacopa Literary Review*, 2014, pp. 89–94.

"For Panic: Say Five Things You See, She Said." *New South*, vol. 13.2, 2020, pp. 6-11.

"Gator Bites." *Solstice*, 2013, solsticelitmag.org/content/first-runner-up-gator-bites/.

"Hush." *Under the Sun*, 2015.

"I Want Candy." *Baltimore Review*, 2013, pp. 333–39.

"Rats." *AGNI*, vol. 101, 2025, pp. 166–71.

"Transportation." *Open Windows: An Anthology of Poetry, Fiction & Essays*, vol. 3, 2008, pp. 53–58.

I am grateful for the opportunity to collect and publish these pieces in new forms and among other pieces for context. Thank you to my friend and copyeditor, Lucy Cooper-Silvis, who taught me several things but especially that the American *gray* has an -a, and we'll correct that even though it's not really preferable to the British *grey* with its somehow more lovely -e.

I want to mention the animals and the husband the title points to. First the nonhuman animals who have been some of my very best friends. Cats: George, Gracie, Fauna, Selkie, Sedna; dogs: Barron, Little Girl, Blue, Ollie, Darby; chickens: Rebeaka, Henrietta, Jadzia, Ellen Ripley (I and II), Buffy the Vampire Killer, Joan Jett, Xena Princess Warrior, Ruth Bader Ginsburg, Daisy, Daphne. And then there is the unnamed and untamed wildlife: the crows, the rats, the snakes, the ants, the possums and racoons, the foxes and weasels. The world, real and imagined, is heavily populated, teeming and noisy with animal life and we also animals in it.

My husband, my most intimate best friend, is Chuck (Charles Caldwell Bowie, III), who died April 16/17, 2015. We met in 2000, were married the following year, and had fourteen years afterward, together. He is always in my mind, in my ear, in the corner of my eye, in everything I do and think and say and am. And yet he is nowhere, absolutely nowhere. It is terrifying to lose yourself midstride as I did. I miss him in the way an amputated limb misses its body.

A note on nonfiction. I have recalled things from fifty or more years ago, and sometimes more recently, in the colors they appear to me in memory. Sometimes I have shifted details in order to make the stories what they are to me and not lose them in perfection; sometimes I have changed names or identifying marks to make sure I am not exposing others or claiming to know them outside my own perceptions and capacity to write them. These things are true (a title for this book I briefly flirted with); others may remember differently.

I wrote once about a boat ride my father took us kids and our cousins on at our grandfather's house in New York. I was small, maybe five or six. My brother was on the same boat ride, three years older. He read my description once the piece was published, told me: that was not what it was like at all. Older, more intrepid, he had had a blast, he remembered the ride as loads of fun with his beloved adventurous father—all the cousins having a great time, just an exciting ride. Younger, much more timid, I was existentially terrified, appalled, angry. I felt the boat was sinking slowly. I believed that my sick drunk dad would swamp us.

Same ride, same lake, same characters, same moment. Very different experiences.

I tell my students about this. Then I say: always write the boat ride you had. You can't write anyone else's. Own it, write it, claim your space.

This is my boat ride. Welcome. I hope we make it across the lake together.

CONTENTS

Feeding the Animals

My arm is the color of toast. I have been outside running in the field behind the house. It's lunchtime, my mother butters Wonderbread with mayonnaise, slips meat onto it, sets a lid of bread on top. I put both arms around my mother's legs, my fingers just meeting on the other side. I shake my head to make my eyes adjust to indoors. I've shucked my sandals somewhere outside. I like the cool kitchen terrazzo underfoot, the sand grinding between my dirty toes.

My father is home. My mother's knife slips in and out of the mayonnaise jar, but her mouth makes a line. I can see the back of her neck curving under a chain that catches in the wisps of her hair. Six or seven gold beads dip in and out of the placket of her yellow-checked blouse. Her capris zip up the side at her waist. As she shifts, foot to foot, the zipper-pull on her pants dances. It's nearly at eye level, so I watch it.

"Bologna," I say. I'm asking.

"Ham," she says.

I dislike ham. I don't like mayo either, but I know I won't get a choice. At the table, my little brother in his highchair fusses and rattles and tries to get out. He's buckled in like an astronaut for take-off. It's the only way to keep him still. My older brother washes himself up. My father comes in from the garage where he's been building something, the saw pitching on and off—the sound of the saw and the drill, and sometimes the hammer. His lips clamp around a cigarette. When it burns to the end of his nose, the smoke makes him squint. He wears old khaki shorts, his white vee-neck t-shirt streaked with sawdust and dirt, bilgey with sweat. He comes through the laundry room with his rolled bandana tied around his forehead, stubs out his cigarette in the ashtray by the door, wipes his face with a dish towel. My younger brother gets very quiet in his highchair. I shift around to the other side of my mother, between her legs and the cabinets. My father kisses her on the cheek, ruffles my hair, heads for the bathroom to run water over his neck. His arm-hair is gilded with sawdust. As he passes, my younger brother gets more and more agitated, rocking the highchair until it lifts on its legs. My father ignores him. My mother simply stops making sandwiches until my father's out of view.

Once he's in the bathroom, she sets me aside, picks up a plate. On it, a half-sandwich cut into bits, some chips, a bit of cookie, a small pile of raisins. She sets it on the tray in front of my little brother, pushes his bangs off his forehead. Her wedding set makes a pattern of diamonds on the ceiling above them and he points at them.

"Eat," she says, she almost whispers. "You have to eat." They lock eyes. They are in love with each other. She is the only one he loves.

"Yeah," I say, "you gotta eat." My mother looks over her shoulder at me, her eyes stony. "Yeah," I say, avoiding her looking at me. "You gotta eat because you're so small. And there's food and you have to eat."

"Thank you," she says, "that's enough."

"But he has to eat," I say.

"He knows."

"But if he doesn't clean his place then he will have to sit there until he cleans his place and he won't sit there."

She frowns. My older brother, still with a bandage on his face where he'd gotten stitches falling or fighting or both, races into the room, drags out his aluminum-plastic chair, sits and shifts his huge blue eyes to my mother. "Can I have cookies?" he asks. My mother does not look at him.

"After," she says. She sets a sandwich cut in two triangles, a tumbler full of milk, and a bowl of chips in front of him. He takes a big bite out of the center of one of the triangles and gulps half the milk down. She tops it off from the glass half-gallon in the fridge. My sandwich is cut in threes like I like it, and I have exactly six chips and two cookies. I peel the crust off the center piece, lift the top bread off and ball it up. I set it aside on my plate as if for later. I take the meat out, set that aside. I eat the bottom bread, folded four times. I do not like this sandwich, but I am not allowed not to eat it. I take a chip, put some of the ham on top. I open my mouth to put it there, but instead I drop it in my lap where it lies until I slide it into my pocket.

My older brother rummages around in his chip bowl for more. My mother fills his glass again, points at the sandwich. "No cookies until—"

He bites rapidly at the soft white bits left next to the crusts. No one eats crusts in my family except my father. "More chips?" he says.

"Sandwich," my mother says, pointing at his plate.

She fixes my father's lunch now. He is also having ham, but his sandwich has cheese and lettuce and a cool slice of tomato on each half, the whole thing flattened under her hand and cut in two rectangles. His chips come beside his sandwich on a big plate. She gets a beer out of the fridge, pulls off the tab, pours it foamless into a tall glass, puts the glass and the can next to my father's place, sets his plate down with a fork, napkin, and knife. Bubbles prick and slide against the inside of the glass. Then she refills my brother's chip bowl and gets her own meal, a pile of cottage cheese with half a canned pear on top, and three tiny chocolate candies from her stash in the cupboard. Sometimes her lunch is a cigarette, sometimes a tall glass of vodka that makes her sleepy afterward so that we're all locked out of the house to play until dinner. She watches my little brother who is rocking his head, an emphatic no. He's eaten nothing. He and my mother are listening to the water run in the bathroom, my father clearing his throat, the bathroom door sliding into its pocket. His footfalls.

"Put something into your mouth," she hisses, "you don't have to chew, but put it in your mouth." My little brother turns red with suppressed howling, my older brother doesn't pay attention, my mother, with her fork in her hand, tenses for critique. I peel a bit of bread off another third of my sandwich and ball it up. My older brother has a milk moustache all the way up both cheeks. He is cramming chips in his mouth when my father rounds the corner and sits down. My mother lights a cigarette, taps it off in her ashtray. She does not look at my little brother at all, only at my father the way a bird looks at a snake.

My father pins my older brother in his gaze. It is a golden gaze, an assessing gaze. My brother expects it and basks. "Good lunch." My brother nods, my mother gets up and gets him more milk, more chips. He has finished all but the two vees of his crust which are just bread and not meat.

"Eat your crusts," my father says. My brother ravages his bowl of chips. "Crusts." My father points at my brother's plate with his finger, but he's caught sight of me now and I stop my fingers mashing the ham up into shards. I almost don't breathe. "How's my darling daughter?"

"Fine thank you," I say. I clear my throat. I am about to say something about a seashell I found in the yard when my little brother begins screaming. He rattles his highchair so hard that my mother has to reach over and steady it with her hand. He shifts down into crying, a high-pitched desperate wailing that only threatens to intensify. Both his hands reach out for my mother. He has four or five teeth, his lips drawn back so you can see them like bits of bone lodged sideways in a raw hole in his face. My mother says, "Shush now, it's okay." He cries harder, his dark eyes with their long black lashes squinched shut, baby tears smearing his face.

"He hasn't eaten his lunch." My father has finished half his sandwich. He swallows his beer, finishes pouring the rest of the can into his glass.

My mother gets up, gets another cigarette, lights it. She is not looking at my father. My little brother pitches his wailing louder, higher. My older brother covers an ear.

"Maybe he's not hungry," I say. I eat a chip, drink a little milk, wipe my mouth with the back of my forearm. My father looks at me a moment, his eyes narrowed, judging. I pick up my napkin and wipe my arm. Refold it precisely, keeping my eyes on my placemat.

He turns to my mother, who stands with her cigarette, just waiting for whatever's next. She pats one side of her hair with the hand holding her cigarette. The smoke makes a jaggedy line above her head. My father says, "He has to eat his lunch. Look at him. He's wailing because he's hungry." My little brother is now beating his head on the back of his highchair, a rhythmic thump-rattle, thump-rattle. My mother puts her hand on the chair where his head makes contact. "Stop that," my father says. My little brother doesn't stop it, though he stops wailing entirely, uncannily silent all at once. He opens his eyes, meets my father's gray-blue stare.

Something about his wet, big-eyed gaze, my mother's protective hand, my older brother's half-uttered snicker means my father pops out of his chair all ablaze, the heat of it flaming at me, even. I slide down my chair and under it. My father's hairy legs appear beside my little brother's chair, my mother's legs shifted between his and the legs of the highchair. I can hear my little brother now, his high-pitched whine like a dog's. "Now, he's just a—"

The air stills perfectly. The tray rattles. The plate rattles. My little brother screeches and howls. "Now, he can't eat that all at once." My mother tries instead to reason with my brother: "Honey, honey, just take a bite. A small bite."

Another rattling, more screeching, and then all of the sudden, bits of everything on the floor. The plate after, landing on its edge and rolling into a corner by the sliding glass doors. I make myself into the smallest possible ball and hum to myself, a single note that vibrates my skull.

Nothing else happens. Not for what seems like a very long time.

My mother starts to clean up the floor, kneeling, gathering the bits in her hands, her lit cigarette stuck between her index and second fingers. Her nails are lacquered bright red. I see my older brother get up, walk through the mess to put his plate in the kitchen.

"Leave it alone," my father says. "He can eat it down there."

My mother gets the plate and slides it onto the table, continues to pick the food up off the ground, her arm reaching, gathering, setting it out of sight on the plate on the table. There is a raisin by my foot. I reach out, pick it up, put it in my pocket to set on the table with the rest of my little brother's food. My mother isn't crying. She is saying *Christ, Christ* and then, "Can you get me another cigarette?" to my older brother. She passes the smoking butt to him to tamp out. No one sees me.

My father says, "Leave it. He can eat it—"

My mother interrupts him to say, "You will not make him eat like an animal off the floor. He's a little boy."

My father says, "He's an animal."

My mother continues to pick things up, and then rises, dusts her knees. My father is taller than she and heavier, but she is standing close to him and not moving out of his way. My brother comes back, I guess with the cigarettes. "Put them on the table," she says.

"He's an animal."

"He's your son."

"No son of mine."

I pull my t-shirt over my knees, tuck my head into the collar, and start rocking. My little brother is whimpering. He knows words, I have seen him know words even though he says very little or nothing, nothing to my father ever.

"He's my son then. At least."

"Tell your son to eat. There are starving children. He has no right to waste food."

My little brother pounds his fists on his tray, rocking in his chair. My father says, "Your son needs to stop that." I hear the lighter strike, I smell smoke. I hear my father breathe in and then exhale.

"We should take him back, right now, before it gets any worse," he says. Then he laughs. "I don't think they'll want him either."

My mother says nothing. My little brother goes silent again, she draws a chair up very close to my brother's and sits. My older brother is standing still in the kitchen, I suspect, or maybe he's gone outside again, I can't tell.

The home. Where we all three came from. Different homes, different children.

My mother says to my little brother, "Sweetheart, just a mouthful. For Mama? Just this little bit?"

"He'll have to finish it all."

"I know."

He notices I'm missing, finally. "Where did she go this time?" I don't dare say.

My mother says, "Under the table, like she always is."

"Animals," my father says.

Among Men

In the psychiatrist's office, I felt cocooned. Even the tasteful Monet prints were like warm baths. "I don't feel like talking," I said. "I just feel like watching."

"Watching what?" he said.

"Myself," I answered. Outside the window on the street below, a car shushed by, then a truck. Someone eating on the sidewalk shouted to someone else about the food.

"You know," I said, "My arm doesn't belong to me."

"Umm," he said.

"It doesn't belong to me. Sometimes I have to ask it to do things for me, like 'pick up that book.' When it does, I think to it, 'thank you,' and it thinks back, 'you're welcome.'

"At least," I said, "at least we get along."

***

The cleaner sat on the roof at noon, eating his sandwich and contemplating all the roofs around him as if they were fields of verdant wheat, which in a way they were. In my town they were all made of white tiles that in that climate mildewed and stained easily. Then they had to be cleaned. This was his job. When a roof grew dingy and dark, dirt weeping from one tile to the next underlapping it, the roof man would come by and ring the doorbell. My mother never let him in, only told him she would ask my dad, who would always get out the ladder that night, set it against the gutters, climb to the top in the dusk and take a look. He always checked the same spot, and it was always near dark when he did, so in hindsight it must have looked very dirty to him regardless of its real condition. He always authorized my mother to hire the roof man the next time he showed up, which without fail was within a week of his first appearance.

"I've come to clean," he'd tell her, as if he knew she would say, "He says go ahead." He didn't talk like any other plumber or electrician or tile man I'd ever heard. He talked just like my father, only his voice was a little deeper and my father's more nasal. "I'll be using the water and it'll be a little noisy," the roof man would say. My mother would nod, and he'd turn away to go to work.

He had a little generator. It fascinated me since it stank of gasoline and sounded like a lawn mower very close up. It made little shimmying movements so that at the end of the day it would be several feet from the back of the truck where he had set it and he'd have to haul it into the truck bed from there. It must've weighed a great deal: when he picked it up, his face took on that look of concentration my dad's got when he was working on weekends. I don't know if the face was for me or really the revelation of some inner feeling. I just know I saw it.

This generator powered a water-spraying machine. It was even louder than the generator, but it was on wheels, so it moved more easily. He would fill up the machine, which had a very long hose, longer than my entire street I thought at the time. He'd fill up the machine with water and bleach from a white milk jug he had gotten out of the passenger floorboard where it sat next to his lunch. Then he'd unload the ladder, take the hose up on the roof and begin spraying. He had a bucket and a scrub-brush for the hard parts.

The roof man never talked to me. But he knew I was there, watching him, mostly because he'd have to move the hose around me when I got in the way. Actually he did talk to me, once. He said, "Be careful, this'll burn if it gets on your skin." In answer, I went and hid in the bushes and watched from there, sitting cross-legged, mesmerized. He moved deliberately over the tiles, the rhythm of his arm and back a kind of dance. The sprayer cleared a pattern of boxes or waves, the pattern there, then invisible, disappearing with the dirt.

The last time I remember seeing the roof man, though it couldn't have been the last time he came to the house, he went up, washed the roof, and instead of packing up his things to go, rang the doorbell. My mother, in the yellow gingham apron my grandmother had smocked for her, her hands wet from something, looked out the glass inset in the door first, then opened it. She didn't ask him anything.

"Well," he said. "You need to have your roof fixed."

My mother nodded. It didn't mean *okay*. It meant, *if you say so*.

He pointed to the left side of the house. My mother looked only at him.

"Up there," he said, "there are a couple of loose tiles. One or two cracked ones, too. Is the water coming through when it rains yet?"

"No," she said. "But there's the attic, of course." More words than I think she'd ever said to him.

"Could be," he said, "could be. Looks like the worst part is over the back of the house, near the girl's bedroom." My mother looked at the oak tree behind him.

"Well, that's all then. Let your husband know," he said.

"Thank you," she said.

And he packed up his things and went.

"He said he could fix the roof," my mother said to my father after he'd sat down in the family room that night, full of dinner.

"What's wrong with it?" he said.

"Nothing much, just some loose parts or something. I didn't really understand," she said, "whether it was serious, but he said he'd come back to fix it if we want him to."

"Where is it cracked?" he said. "Any water yet?"

He got up and checked all the ceilings. I watched as my mother effortlessly herded him towards my room in the back, west-facing corner of the house. There was nothing on my ceiling that I could see. It was flat and white, only a little shadowed by the lamp.

"Hmm. I wonder if there's water in the attic," he said.

That Saturday, my father and my brother went up on the newly cleaned roof to look for the damage. I watched from the ground as they worked back from the front porch, talking to each other as they went. I couldn't hear what they were saying, only I knew they were saying roof things because my father would grab my brother occasionally and point to something. They'd both look, consult one another, then move another few feet towards the back. When they got above my room, they stopped. My father crouched on the tiles in a flat place very near the peak of the roof where the back wing projected into the yard. My brother bent down and put his hands on his thighs. They were looking so closely at the roof that its whiteness cast up light around them and they seemed like cutout figures against the trees next door.

My dad lifted a tile which broke in half in his hands. They both came to the front of the house and down the ladder. My father got a black tarp and took it back up, covering the broken tiles with it to keep out the rain. Uphill of the break, he attached it with tape. Downhill, he tucked the edges under.

When the roofer came back the next week, my mother opened the door before he rang.

"Saturday?" she said.

"Yes, of course," he said. "I see there's a tarp up there now, that's good. No water in the bedroom, so Saturday's fine."

She nodded and closed the door.

They all three went up on the roof together. My father and brother removed the tarp. The roofer carried up some of the new tiles, my brother carried up the others. They didn't talk much, only pointed at things mostly. It was hot like it was most days, hotter on the roof that much closer to the sky and without trees for shade or bleach-water for coolness. In a matter of a few minutes, my father and brother had removed their shirts. Their backs looked dirty brown compared to the roof, my father's breasts when he bent over pointed downwards. My brother was tight like a cigar, nothing changed when he bent over. The bandana my father wore to keep the sweat from his eyes looked like a red rubber band around his head. High clouds scudded around above them, but never seemed to cross paths with the sunlight. They were all hot together. It was taking longer than they wanted it to.

When I got to the top of the ladder, I could not look down. It seemed too far to look, sort of like I was at the edge of the gutter and watching myself from the bushes simultaneously. It made me a little dizzy to be up there on the roof, only I wasn't really, I was stuck on the end of the ladder because I couldn't figure out how to get on the roof itself, proper. I had watched the men do it, lean into their upper bodies, hands palm-down flat on the edge of the roof, then one leg over the gutter, sneaker flat to the tiles, push up and to the right into a crouch and from there to standing. I had my hands right, I guessed, I was leaning right into them, I guessed, only I couldn't get my leg up. The ladder wobbled under my left foot. It must have made a noise.

"She can't come up here," said my brother. His face was red with heat. "She'll fall and get killed."

"No, she won't," said my father. "It's okay."

"I can't," I said, panting a little, my hands on the edge of the tiles. "I can't get my leg up."

"If you can't get your leg up, you can't come up here," said my brother.

"Can too," I said. I swung my right leg as high as it would go. The ladder wobbled wildly. My leg stayed in midair. The ground looked messy and green behind me.

"Help me," I said.

My father came over and took me by the arms, hoisting me free of the ladder and into the air above the rooftop. For a second I was where none of them had been, higher even. Then I was on the roof. I stood behind them as they worked, then sat on the edge of the pile of tiles, my knees up under my chin, watching. Sometimes I would take a tile from beside or beneath me and hold it while they worked. Sometimes they would take it from me and say thank you. Sometimes they would take one from the pile without noticing the one I had. On the ground below us lay the tarp and the broken pieces of roof they had thrown there for cleaning up later. I walked around behind my father to look at them, then took a broken tile from the roof and threw it down with the others. It made a satisfying plop-crunch noise. I threw another, discovered how I could help, and began getting rid of the pulled-up tiles in rhythmic bursts. *Duh dah duh daaaah daaaaaa! Plop-crunch, plop-crunch. Duh dah dah dah daaaah Duh dah plop-crunch.* I danced my behind to the beat, imagining nothing but the music of falling, breaking tiles.

I began to get hot, sticky sweaty hot. My hair in its twin braids stuck to my face and neck, sweat crept down behind my knees. I looked at the men around me, my father and brother sweating into the air, their backs open to catch breezes. I suddenly realized how much cooler I could be if I just got rid of my clothes. I sat down, crossed my arms in front of my body and held on to the hem as my mother had taught me to do to get off my shirt. I looked at the sky, clear and blue and potentially full of birds.

The roof man coughed. My father looked up.

"Leave your shirt on," he said.

"But I'm hot," I said.

"Leave your shirt on," he said.

"Leave it on," said my brother. "What are you, stupid?"

"No," I said. "I'm hot. You have yours off."

"Can't take your shirt off up here," said my father. "Only in the house."

"You have yours off," I said to my brother.

"You're not a boy," he said.

"Am so," I said. "Neither are you. I can take my shirt off."

They all stared a moment then went back to work.

"Am so," I said to no one. "I can if I want to."

I sat for a while as my brother swore, scraping and cutting his hands, as my father and the other man lifted and lay the tiles, silent and diligent. In a little while, I edged my way towards the ladder, hoping they wouldn't notice my leaving, picking up leaves and inspecting them, watching a blue jay in the pine watch me. I got down the ladder without help. Then I went inside and took my shirt off, then my shorts and sneakers. I got down a book about a man who walked across the surface of the moon, falling sometimes into craters, and soon enough fell asleep on the floor, nearly naked and dreaming. While I slept they fixed the roof so the rain wouldn't come in, and the roofer, after shaking my father's hand, put his tools in the truck, backed up the driveway and went home into the afternoon.

***

"Is it only your arm that doesn't belong to you?" he asked.

I don't know, I thought. *Does it matter?*

"Yes," I said. "Only the right arm. I'm awful at tennis, of course."

One of his plants was dying. I saw this as a terrible commentary on his abilities. I mean if you can't keep a philodendron alive, what business do you have trying to help people?

"It needs more water," I said. "When did you repot it last?"

He looked over his shoulder at the windowsill. Then back at me.

"Actually," he said, "I'm better at cactuses. Why do you think your right arm doesn't belong?"

I don't know, I thought. *Isn't it just arbitrary?*

"Because that's the one I write with," I said.

Transportation

I don't know where they got that station wagon. My mother told me she barely remembers it, only that sometime in the 1970s the cat had kittens in the back. *What a mess*, she said, laughing. But I remember it clearly, how it smelled like hot plastic and baby food, how the light stopped on the dusty dash, how at night with the interior lights on, we were projected onto the windshield like in a mirror. My father let me drive sitting in his lap though my hands didn't fit around the wheel under his, though I could only just glimpse over the dashboard the road running under the long stretch of hood out in front with a bright dot of sun on it. I remember the bench seats under my thighs, stuck to them in the heat, how the seats left the imprint of their tuck-marks on the backs of my legs. I remember the rasp of the dry nap on the floor mats against my knees as I jammed a hand under the seats, looking for lost pennies. I can see even the black plastic handles on the doors, even the way the speedometer needle vibrated with road rumble when we went fast or over speed bumps or into dips. I know it was red, deep merlot red, and being a family car, that it had decorous fins and understated chrome. But mostly I remember being trapped in it for days in 1967, when my parents, my two brothers and I, our cat and my mother's fine china moved south, all together, all in one long road trip.

My father had gotten a new job in Florida, land of flowers we had no names for, a place my mother never wanted to live. She told my father she'd come and bring us—therefore, that he could take this position he'd been offered—only after she'd seen Belleair. The little town didn't quite remind her of her home in Pennsylvania but was at least not a jungle or a Levittown in cinderblock painted pastel pink or blue, all the lawns rectangles of gravel or weeds. Sometime in early August that year, the movers appeared on our doorstep, loaded up everything in our house in New Jersey, and shut the doors hard. We stuffed into the station wagon whatever they didn't pack in the truck for the two- or three-day drive to our new house. My older brother arranged the boxes in the back into an igloo, the space inside just fitting his body. We could barely see out the rear window. I was three; my younger brother was just an infant, my older brother, only six and a half.

Mostly it's hot that summer, and against all reason, we're not going to Cape Cod or the mountains. Instead, we're heading south as fast as we can go, straight into blazes. My mother rides shotgun, I'm in her lap, my father drives. My older brother naps the whole way with his comic books between the boxes in the way-back, the cat spooning with him in the too warm dimness. My younger brother bubbles drowsing in the back, strapped loosely into a car seat; periodically he writhes in his sleep and sends the contraption into rocking and high, mousy squeaks. Awake he writhes always, fists restless, legs kickkicking, body a snake on hot pavement. This annoys my father nearly into a rash. When the baby sleeps, we all inhale relief like cool mountain air. As we drive southward, the radio plays The New Christy Minstrels, my father says something, my mother murmurs *Uh-huh*, not listening. The hair on his arms filters the wind coming through his window, his forearm crisping in the sun. The skin peels up later, and I get to pick at it, at the flakes and the long strips of opaque membrane. The freckles don't come up but instead stick to the tender pink-brown new skin that stays behind. My father's cigarette fumes in the ashtray, a thread moving in the sunlight when we're stopped. I can't see past his dark glasses to his eyes, but then I don't really want to. He doesn't interest me.

I'm focused on watching my mother, instead. She smells like licked metal and underarm deodorant and Aquanet and toothpaste. She isn't smoking at the moment, so her lipstick is perfect, a pink shape like a kiss. She sings some with the radio, a finger tapping her leg. Her arms rest next to her on both sides, one elbow against the door, pressing it a little. Now and then she reaches back to check my brother, to test the straps and adjust his clothing or his pacifier, to make sure he's still sleeping. I can feel the light on my leg in a single patch like a hand, the subtle vibration through my whole body that tells me I'm in a car that's moving. The road unravels beneath us, the sun on our left in the morning.

We pass fruit stands with peaches and tomatoes in piles. "Dirt cheap," my father says, "Let's stop and get some." The edge of the Appalachians slips by on the horizon, blue shoulders steaming, always on our right. We get gas and the men check the oil, run a rag over the windshield. My father pays them and they wave at us as we go. The places we stay have funny names like Ramada and Curtis Nighty-Night Hotel. The first night we get a room with a Magic Fingers vibro-massage bed. With a quarter, my brother and I make the bed jiggle, take turns lying on it and watching our stomachs shake around. We drink glasses of water until we're distended, swallow air to make space, then vibrate so we can listen to the sloshing. I lay my head on the hump of his flat, tight stomach and hear a milk jug being shaken, which makes me wonder. I say, "I wonder," and we discover that if we talk while the machine's running, we sound funny, like talking into a fan. So we say everything we can think of, then shout to see if we still sound funny loud. My mother shushes us; my father is out for ice right then there's no one to yell at us yet. My older brother takes his quarter, drops it in the slot and lies smack in the middle of the chenille bedspread, which is now all bunched up with our rolling around on it. He hums, then says quietly "Poop-poop-poop-poop" so only I can hear. It sounds double funny with the quaver; this makes me convulse onto the floor in giggles and notice how the ceiling has sponge-marks in the plaster.

We feed the machine so many quarters that my father, who's back from getting ice, finally gets irritated, yells, takes away our change, then turns on the TV loud enough so we'll listen and stop clowning around. We watch *Hee Haw* and Lawrence Welk while he makes drinks with the ice he's brought. The room smells like someone else's house, musty and alcoholic. When he's finished, we go to the Stuckey's across the way where I get a hamburger, eat part of it, and give the French fries to my brother who stuffs two in his nose to make me laugh, which I do. The waiter brings us extra pop, with straws, but before we're completely finished, my mother leaves in the car with the baby, whose food's gone all cold; he sicks up on my mother's shoulder, on a spare diaper, something curdy and yellow. My father and brother and I walk back. In the hotel room, we turn the TV to something else, a movie maybe, and lie on our stomachs to watch on the vibrating bed (which is still now), our sneakers in a neat row by the closet, our stockinged feet pointed at the pillows. On the other bed, my baby brother cries and crawls around and craps himself. He stinks of misery and diapers. My mother puts them in the toilet at night, then into a bag in the morning, rinsed but not clean. His face goes tomato red when he screams, then white. The heat flattens his sweaty black hair. His fists rub his eyes until the lashes stick together in thick wads like paintbrushes. He cries and cries and cries and drives us all itchy.

On the second day in the car, we pass nothing but fields of cotton and heat-blurred telephone poles. My mother sighs heavily, sweats, sighs some more. Sometimes the radio plays and she sings, sometimes there's just static or preachers and my father shuts it off. Right now, it plays The New Christy Minstrels, my mother says *Uh-huh* to something my father's talking about, my father smokes his cigarette, sets it in the tray, smokes it, crushes it out into a bent lump when he's done, the filter a yellow spot at the end. The smoke rises in a thread in the sunlight, disperses in a fat cloud that fills the car and makes the light into something living. Bored and sweaty, tired of the trees and the poles and the fields of green with white blobs of cotton rushing by, I want a story. I want something else to do but sit. I lean forward over my mother's knees and run my finger across the letters above the glovebox. I say to my mother, "What does this say?" She glances at the word, looks away again out the window, says what it says for me. I wait two beats. Then, "What does this spell?" She says the word again, not looking, not understanding. I wait a few more beats, push against her blouse hard enough that she's paying attention now, and look up into her face. "No, Mommy, what are the letters?" So she spells it. We do this again, say it, spell it, again, the cotton fields passing, the telephone poles passing, the song changing to something else. My father smokes another cigarette, watches the road and the other drivers, one hand idling on the wheel, the other dangling by its wrist by the blinker knob.

I am three years old. My mother says: *Pontiac.* She spells: *P-O-N-T-I-A-C.* My father looks over, looks away, decides this isn't bothering him, smokes another cigarette and dials the radio to get a new station. The road passes underneath us, outside the window, the same road, much the same scenery. We are getting somewhere, it just doesn't seem that way.

I'm three years old. I can talk very well and know that words are something I say, that get me cookies or a spanking or a trip to the shore. I have learned my *abc*'s (*won't you sing along with me?*) so I know my letters, and I don't mess up the middle part either (*L-M-N-O-P*). I just don't know that one is the other, that letters make words. I make no real connection between *Pontiac* and *P-O-N-T-I-A-C,* but saying them out loud right then together seems not boring, not cotton and telephone poles and the road rushing by. So I make her repeat them again, again, again. She sighs, checks my brother, shifts me to one side to lift a leg off the vinyl with a ripping, wet sound that smells of talcum. Her gauzy headscarf is patterned with big blue flowers; it's tied under her chin and the ends waggle in the breeze like fingers or leaves. I can't see her eyes when I look at the letters over the glovebox. I have to turn around to see her, which I do because I realize that looking at her means she'll say the word again. I say, "What does this say, spell it," and she does. Patiently. Many times. I lose count, can't count that high, forget to count. She is the best mother I've ever had.

And then she's done. "No more saying for now," and from her purse on the floor she gets me a cookie, one of those with the hole in the middle that just fits my index finger. She lights a cigarette, puts on her sunglasses, watches the cotton, the telephone poles, the lines running down the middle of the road. But I'm still fixated on the letters. I nibble my cookie, keeping all the sides even, and rub the letters with the other hand, not absent-mindedly. Under my hand are the *P* and the *O*. I trace them with one finger, over and over. I hear my mother say: *Pontiac.* I trace the *N*, the *P*, the *O*, then I smooth them all away with one sideways motion of my hand. I finish the cookie and get the wet washcloth from the plastic bag in her purse wiped over my hands, both of them, erasing everything like a wet-clean blackboard. I lean forward once I'm all dry and my mouth cleaned too, and retrace them, listen to my mother's voice in my head saying: *Pontiac. Pontiac. Pontiac.* I lean back against her chest, the sunlight lying on my cheek, and hum a little tune, then sing it on *Lalala,* then sing the letters (*P-O-N-T-I-A-C*) for a while, under my breath. I sing the word after that, out loud, with feeling. I begin to dance *Pontiac* with my head and shoulders and butt, emphasizing every other letter, every other syllable. My mother watches the road, sighs, shifts me to her other leg, wishes out loud that I'd be still. "It's nearly lunch," she says to no one in particular though my father is listening, "We should stop." My little brother fusses, and my mother reaches back again.

The red station wagon with my brothers and me in it and the cat who sleeps with my older brother in the way-back, and the luggage that shifts around when we drive into rest stops and take bologna sandwiches and pop out of the green aluminum Coleman cooler is south of Macon somewhere, in the flat where the stands of pulp wood interrupt the cotton fields that interrupt the stands of pulp wood. We're nearly to Florida, land of flowers and white sand beaches, not yet land of Disney. I understand only that when we get there, I will see palm trees and dolphins maybe, and I think it's a vacation, not the rest of my life. I wonder to myself if people in Florida will speak another language than mine (I'm convinced my

Pennsylvania-Irish grandmother doesn't speak the same one I do and she's not half so far away as Florida). I think about what we'll eat there, and whether my friends can come play once we get my toys out of the back. I am rubbing the word *Pontiac* over the glovebox and thinking about palm trees, my grandmother's voice, the taste of bologna and butter and cold pop when under my hand the feel of the raised plastic letters becomes sound and vision almost blindingly unbidden and quick, like the lift of a yawn under the sternum. I hear the *P* and feel it under my hand and hear *PPP* and know somehow that the next sound which is *O-N* should be on and know that the *T* under the very tip of my pointer finger now sounds like scolding, sounds like the staccato hissing drip of the faucet at home which is now somewhere in the past behind us, the road eating it, kicking it behind, gone (*Stee, stee, stee*), that the rest is an animal from one of my picture books of the zoo, nothing I'll ever see at home, a cow with curving horns and long-grassy hair that gives milk the color of the sky (*Yak*) and that all of this together is my mother's voice saying: *Pontiac*. This comes to me like a snapshot all in red, taken with a flash attachment. I see the word (*PONTIAC*), I hear it (*Pontiac*). I feel it zipping around a corner down my spine, the worn silver-tone letters on red vinyl flying through South Georgia somewhere, shadow interrupting dazzled sunlight. The pines lean out over the road to shoulder their *P*s and *N*s into my brand-new, one-word lexicon, leafing out into those other words I will learn, the bumps in the road suddenly meaningful, readable, something I might understand, the world suddenly filled with words, not things. I sit very still. I say: "Pontiac," half-whispering, finger tracing, no question mark. My mother shifts beneath me, "Yes, Pontiac. P-O-N-T-I-A-C. Jesus," she says, lighting another cigarette and squinting into the windshield.

Dogfish

"Hey," he said. "Do you know what a dogfish is?"

"No," I said.

"Me neither."

He stood behind me on the sandy patch just at the back edge of the concrete sea wall. He bent over my head to see down into the water. The shadow he cast was loose at the edges where the water moved. It spread out over everything, mixing with the shadow of the bridge briefly, then separating itself when he leaned back a little. I didn't look at him directly, since I'd have to squint into the sun to do that, and besides, my business was crabbing and the crabs were in the water below my feet. In any case, looking back into the sun I'd see nothing, everything would be just a blur of light. So I looked down at his shadow, at the water. I held my end of an old cotton string wound loosely around my hand. It ran a white line downwards, bending where it met the water. I could see straight down to the junk on the bottom. A beer bottle. Someone's sneaker. Broken things that glittered. The water washed silt and algae back and forth, back and forth. The sea wall hurried the tide outwards into the Gulf of Mexico.

"Catching anything?"

I put my hand on the cooler next to my leg, rocked it loosely to show him it was empty. "Just got here."

"Been watching you for a while," he said, though I knew that couldn't have been true. So I said nothing, so he said nothing. Instead we watched a boat slip through the channel a little too far out to tell who was driving. I could see a dark head, some hair. The boat itself was fast, white, too loud, useless for fishing. It hit waves with a *pashboom pashboom*, hollow, just hitting the top of things, impatient like that to be somewhere else. It left a wake I knew would rock the water up against the jetty and then the sea wall I sat on. It silted up my line with its raw chicken neck tied to the end. I lifted the neck off the bottom and washed it clean. The water was warming. The meat left a little grease on the surface. I had my net ready.

"Been watching you for a while," he said again, still looking towards the boat. "I wanted to know if you knew what dogfish are, but I guess you don't."

"Look," I said. "Stone crab." A beigey-brown crab shoving invisible bits of nothing into his mouthparts shifted out from under a piece of smashed concrete. He skittered this way and that, picking at things with his black-tipped claws. He wasn't interested yet in the chicken.

The man shuffled closer up behind me, his shadow shortening as he bent over the water, close enough that I could see his shoes just behind my leg. Dark leather ones, with socks. That meant he didn't live here. No old men wore shoes if they lived here, only plastic sandals you could hose the sand out at the end of the day. Though I didn't look at him, I knew he was old. He talked old, like my grandfather. The crab under my feet twitched and scrambled some.

"Looks like a blue to me."

"Nope," I said. "Stone."

"Huh." He backed away, then, his shadow disappearing. As he walked, his feet brushed on the grass. A breeze came and a cloud covered the sun for a minute. I lost the bottom of the water under my feet, but when it passed, I saw the end of my string again, the chicken neck like a pale toy, the meaty edges fringy and mobile in the wash.

I was no fool. I knew all about dogfish. Everyone did. They hid under the bridge and would get you if you swam there. You never did see dogfish, really. Couldn't catch them, couldn't eat them. You knew where they were because at the end of the day, you'd send your waste-bait under there and they'd take it. The line would float a little and then be shaken to bits in the dark. You'd pull it up, loose and ragged and spent. The bait always gone, only a loop left at the end to show where it had been. Sometimes we did that to get rid of bad bait. For fun. To see if it would come out of the dark and eye us straight on.

The man came back in just a little while with a lawn chair and a soda for himself. He didn't ask if he could sit with me, but then he didn't really sit with me. Just behind me in the grass, in the shade of a few scabby pines and a gumball tree. I watched the line go down, danced it a little just to send the meat smell into the water. The wavelets lapped against the wall, the hard sparks of sun rushing upwards on the peaks. A barnacle emerged, waved its fringes, six or seven more did the same. I scratched my ear, my shadow shifting on the water, and they snapped shut like beaks. The chicken neck at the end of my line settled on a jar on the bottom. I put the line between my toes because I liked the feel of it.

"Do you eat the crabs?" the man asked.

The water lapped against the sea wall. A school of needlefish hovering in my shadow floated up and down. Walnut jellyfish stuck in the slight current wandered in and out of view. I could see a storm coming in, far away, swinging right to left, like they always did. I imagined I heard thunder. The curtain of rain on the horizon was green and gray and made the edge of the water where it met the sky dissolve. I looked away, pretended to ignore him, thought about whether the ants I was sitting next to would bite me. Decided on an answer.

"Nope, I don't."

"Really?"

"Nope. Can't stand them." I jiggled the rope with my toes, sending a crab who'd been edging closer scuttling away fast.

"So what do you do with them?" he asked.

"I put them to sleep. Then I take them home and my dad eats them."

The man shifted in his lawn chair, the plastic webbing creaking against the aluminum frame. He tossed something past me into the water, a peanut shell maybe, that spiraled down out of sight, pale in the deeper water. Across the inlet on a finger of land circled by more sea wall, a woman in a house-dress and curlers flipped a carpet in her backyard. The grass was so green and close-clipped that it looked fake. The carpet snapped like rigging. She went indoors, snicked the sliders closed, and locked them.

When I saw the crab right under my feet on top of the meat—mouthparts like fans, claws moving left and right like boxing, like two shovels feeding a conveyor—I eased my shadow off the water and leaned back, one hand feeling for my net, the handle warm from the sun. Then I pulled the line slowly closer to the surface, close enough that I could swing the net up under. He was out of the water and fighting in a flash, his claws dripping water and bits of meat, closing and unclosing in the net. His eyes, balled up on the sides of his head, were blind as seeds.

I pulled the line and neck out of the net, intent now, the man behind me as good as gone. I tangled the net in the crab's claws, let him think he was doing some good with them, then flipped him over on his back. His legs swam the air. Then, as I'd been taught, I rubbed the triangle on his white belly with my forefinger, crooned a song because that seemed like the thing to do. The crab felt slick and cool, more fragile than seashells, more alive. Seashells were just bones, pieces of skeletons that shaped things long dead, long eaten. A living crab felt different, like it had a mind at least for freedom. I leaned over the net, stroking and crooning and pretty soon between the song and my forefinger, the crab began to go off somewhere in its head. His legs stopped moving and relaxed, his claws stopped scrabbling the net. When he seemed fast asleep, I got the net free, picked him up by his limp-legged body, and set him in the cooler.

When I glanced at the old man at last, he had that slack face people get when they see you do something they think you can't do, no one can do, and you've just done it. *What do you know?*—that face.

"Where'd you learn that?"

"Friend taught me."

"Oh," he said.

"Wanna see a dogfish?" I said.

"There're dogfish here?"

"Sure, right there, under the bridge."

He got up out of the chair to come look, stood so close I could smell him now, the way all the old men smelled, like they never showered enough or let their clothes dry all the way. I pointed at the dark water under the lowest part of the bridge. Three sheepsheads schooled under my feet. I watched their stripes matching and unmatching the light playing on the seabed.

"Sheepsheads," I said. "Three. Right there." Pointing down at my feet.

"Boney."

"Yep, no good catching them. Pretty big though."

"Seen bigger," he said, rocking on his toes and looking into the water.

A lady showed up about that time, crossing the lawn between the pines. She wore shorts and plastic sandals and had that haircut my mom's friends wore that meant they were moms.

"Whatchall doing?" she asked.

"Looking for dogfish," he said. "Under the bridge. There in the dark."

"Hmm," she said. "You can't see dogfish, you know that."

"This kid puts the crabs to sleep," he said, "and feeds them to people like that."

"What?" she said, looking at me. I looked at her blouse, not in her face. I could see which direction her chin went, that she was watching him mostly. I felt bad for him. "Puts crabs to sleep?" she said.

"Yep," I said. "To sleep."

"That's a wonder," she said. I think she was laughing.

"Rubs their bellies," he said.

"What do you know," she said.

I sat down again with my line to let them work this one out. Only now I didn't know what to do—show her? Not show her? I waited for her to leave, jiggled the crabs off the line when they came. She went back in after a while with the empty Coke bottle, and I settled the chicken neck back into the water. Later, it got dark under my feet and it was time to go. I couldn't see the bottom anymore and I felt like I needed my dinner. I got up, looked him in the face.

"Gotta go," I said. His nose was burnt a little, but he had blue eyes.

"Not much luck today," he said.

"Nope."

"Used to get a lot of blues out of here."

"I never did."

"Hmm," he said. I heard him get up, fold his chair.

"Dogfish are sharks," he said. "You know. See you another time, I suppose. Nice talking to you." He walked off over the grass and into the back of a low, stucco-sided house painted mint-green. I could see him moving past the windows into some darkened room toward the front. A flock of pelicans lofted over the roof tiles, but he was inside now and didn't see them.

Dogfish are sharks. Of course I knew. Everyone did, only you called the ones that hid in the shadows dogfish, not sharks. Sharks were the ones swimming in the open, like the hammerheads we saw from the boat or the nurse sharks, or the great whites on TV. I was no fool. I knew what dogfish were. I knew where to find them, too. When I was certain he was inside, I let the line out under the bridge and waited for the tug, which came. Then I whipped the line onto the grass and rolled it up, put it in my tiny tackle box and spit out the raw bacon I'd been chewing all day. It bobbed in the current moving to where the sun was going down. The woman across the inlet came out with a drink, sat down in a chair by herself to watch the water. The ice made brittle sounds banging against the glass. Before I left, I opened the cooler toward the sea wall and let the crab go, then shook it hard over the water to make sure it was empty.

I Want Candy

The car sat there some days for hours without shade. The driver's head was a black lollipop resting on the seatback, sometimes straight up, turning to watch us. I liked to hang upside-down on the monkey bars. I liked the way my shirt fell down to my armpits, the way the air felt on my stomach, how the little heat gathered where the cloth bunched. I liked to feel my ponytail rocking against my head. I liked to sway like a swing, my thighs pushing against the bar. My hands stretched out over my head didn't touch the ground. I liked to watch the car sitting there by the curb, the shadow of the person inside watching back all upside down, the car on the ground in the sky, the head a drop of pendulous dirty oil.

We had known since kindergarten about these cars. Our teachers told us that they were filled with candy of all kinds, chocolate softened to butter in the heat, chocolate we could lick off each finger, one at a time, the sand and the taste of the metal bars and the childish sweat all mingled. There was chocolate in that car, we knew it, stacks and stacks of it there in the back seat. And Sweet Tarts and Now-and-Laters and Tootsie Pops. Peppermint sticks like at Christmas, only the soft kind that fell into pure sugar in our mouths. We knew what was in that car, parked there where we played every day. We hung from our bars and gossiped with our Barbies, our eyes flicking over and over to the candy store set up right there waiting for us to come to the window, get in and take what we wanted.

As it sometimes was, the car was sitting there parked by the curb before we came out to play that morning. It had been painted green like the pin oak leaves behind it, only it had faded in the sun to the color of salt-water taffy. We never saw it leave, it just sat there, the dark rectangle of shadow underneath it shifting slightly is all. By afternoon, the whole car simmered, poured out heat from its hood, from the long, finned side panels that ended in two red lights. The house on the other side of the street wavered like a mirage when we looked through the heat at it. I flipped down, my legs swinging around the pendulum of my head. The gray sand underneath, ringed with prickers Bobbie's brothers hadn't bothered to mow, caught me up, squelched up between my fingers. I stood up, looked up at the bars, the sun making star-patterned dazzles on the hot metal.

"I'm getting candy," I said.

Bobbie and Janie looked at me. Bobbie sat on top, on the rounded dome, her Barbie in one hand, a plastic doll-sized comb in the other. Janie had arranged herself so she was lying flat out across the bars, her hips in their red private-school kiltie hanging down. She'd been to church-school in the morning and snuck out without changing to play-clothes. She polished a bar with the back of her white knee socks. She'd painted her fingernails apple-red, but that was a week ago and now each one had only a bar of color across it, chipped on the edges like a continent. She'd pronged her Barbie upright on a bar so she didn't have to hold her. She was naked and her head sat backwards and askew on her neck. Earlier that day, inside with the TV going, I'd told Janie and Bobbie to draw elephants for a while. Bobbie's Barbie, stuck in the crook of her arm while she colored, wore an evening dress with spangles. We'd taken Ken's head off this morning, put it in a box with Skipper and some plastic dog. We had no idea what happened to Ken's body and didn't care.

"I'm getting some candy," I said again. I dusted my hands on my shorts but the sand stuck and rasped between my fingers. I headed for the hose, turned it on. The water poured out, hot and stinking of sulfur like all our hose-water did.

Janie dropped her head way back between her shoulders, her eyes rolling up so that she could see the hedge behind the monkey bars upside down.

"What kind?" Bobbie asked. The water sluiced over my fingers and into the grass like a heavy rain. I took a mouthful, spit it on the side of the house.

"Pop Rocks," I said.

"They have spider eggs in them," Janie said.

"That's Bubblicious. Not Pop Rocks." Bobbie went back to arranging Barbie's hair. I stood with my hands on my hips. I pointed.

"I'm asking that guy for some candy."

Bobbie and Janie didn't even look. Janie's left leg kicked up, Bobbie concentrated on a hard knot at the back of Barbie's head, which had come off in her hand. She flipped it over, the neck hole to the sky, the better to get at the knot.

"Can't do that," Janie said to the sky.

"Well, I am." I put my hands on my hips, made fists like my older brother did, the sand grinding between my fingers. No one said anything else. Bobbie looked at the Barbie head in her hand, then at the car. A strand of her hair was sweated dark and stuck to her forehead.

I turned my back on them. Behind me, I heard Bobbie drop to the ground, so I turned around again to wait for her. She tucked Barbie's head in her shorts, the hair sticking out of her pocket like corn silk. Bobbie was tall, her legs were awkward and long and had freckles spattered all over them. Her knees looked like fat beads. She seemed older than seven, her face losing its baby roundness already. She had two green barrettes shaped like frogs clipped in her white-blond hair, one above her temple on either side of her bright pink part. A purple wristwatch hung like a bracelet on her left arm. Bobbie dusted her hands on her shorts, hitching one hip forward then the other as she walked, the better to get at the cloth on the seat of her pants. She looked at her palms, spread her fingers. The dirt made gray streaks between them.

"Hey," said Janie behind us. "Hey." We ignored her. She stayed where she was.

Unlike some of our neighbors, we didn't then have St. Augustine grass, that intensely green, thick sod that buries you to your ankles, makes the ground feel like it's padded and deep and wants to pull you down or trip you up or keep you from moving. Bobbie's yard was sand, crabgrass, whatever grew in the salty loose soil. We skimmed over it like bats.

The man in the car watched us coming, his head turned towards us as always. Nothing shifted except the bigness of things, the car growing like a loaf, the man's head filling more space, the car and the man pushing out the lush margin of the neighborhood around them. I could see him clearly now, his brown eyes, the way his dark-blond hair stood up straight on his head the same way my brother's did in the summer, the fan of it at the crown where it grew in a swirl. I could see his teeth just between his lips. He smiled at us, his eyes now half closing, his smile now weird and straight, not a curve. The black spots of his nostrils looked like holes in his face. His shoulder shook and shook.

"Mister," I said.

Bobbie halted a good six feet from the car, but I didn't know. So I came on. "Mister. Hey Mister." He said nothing, just watched me, his eyes flicking between me and Bobbie, his teeth like dots between his lips, his smile straighter and straighter. "Hey, have you got Pop Rocks?" I said. I came right up to the open window, laid my forearm across the hot metal, framed my face in the window like my mother did when she talked to friends in parking lots, her head just outside their cars, her arms holding the bag of things she'd bought or the baby.

This close I could smell the car, the heat and the oil and the dashboard cracked and cooking in the sun. The man in the car smelled salty and warm like the cat's fur when it'd been lying all day in the heat. His beard was coming in and I knew that if I touched it, it would sound like my father's did when he rubbed his hand across it in the morning before coffee. The man's t-shirt had been sweated through at the neck like jewelry, a collar of dark blue above the lighter blue. The shirt said something, "Property of" something, but my eyes slid down over the words. I could see inside the car, see the bench seat in front with its vertical stripes sewn in, dark green vinyl, see the rip on the passenger side. There was a newspaper open beside his naked leg, one edge lapped over his thigh. It had an advertisement from a local store, the gray paper deckled at the edge, the hair on his thigh caught in the deckle. He had one hand resting in his lap. He had one hand on his penis. He was breathing the smell of old cigarettes into the car so that watching I sensed how it was inflating like a balloon, stretching thin and huge and if I just waited it would float away into the blue-metal sky.

"Touch it," he said.

"What?"

"Hey," said Bobbie, her voice loud, high, and shaky. "Hey you, perv."

He didn't look at her. I watched his shoulder shake, his right hand pumping up and down, the way the head of his penis appeared and disappeared into his palm. His left hand, a charmed snake, came up and out the window. It smelled of metal and dirt. It smelled of vinyl and Johnson's lotion and Coca-Cola. It was inches from my face, it was clean and pale and one blue vein threaded through the hairs across its back.

"Touch it," he said.

His fingertips settled behind my ear, there on my hair. I could feel the edges of his fingers on my earlobe, the way my earlobe fitted between them, the way the fingers lay there without pressure at all or asking anything. "Ah," he breathed.

Behind me, Bobbie stumbled a few steps forward, grabbed me by the elbow, her fingers digging in. My left arm swung away from my body, hinged at the shoulder the way my head was hinged at my ear. I knew what I was looking at. I had brothers. He didn't scare me. He had candy and I wanted it, I deserved it. Bobbie pulled lightly like a reminder of what my arm was. "Come on," she said, "Come on."

His head rolled away from me, rolled against the seat, rolled and rolled. His neck looked loose and stringy. His shoulder shook faster and faster. I stopped watching to check the back seat. I could see some books there, an empty Coke can, a pair of women's sandals, a rolled up umbrella. Nothing like what I expected, no boxes, no bars, no bags full of Dum-dums. Where was it?

Nothing in the front seat, nothing on the floorboards. Nothing anywhere. Not even a stray wrapper.

He didn't have candy, he never had candy, he never would have candy.

I was an idiot.

"Come on," Bobbie said. "Leave him alone."

She pulled my arm again. I stumbled back a step, my sneaker catching on the curb. His hand jostled loose. It gripped the window frame like it needed to hold something, anything. His fingernails looked like little shells, white and pink.

"But I want candy," I said. "Where is the candy?"

Far off, the afternoon thunderheads grumbled. I could smell the bay, the mudflats at low tide just a block or so away. Sweat dripped from under my braid, rolled down straight to the waistband of my shorts. The man should have had candy. Everyone said he did.

I leaned into the window again, like I needed to tell him something important. "It isn't fair," I growled at him, intent on making him listen. "Where is the candy? You're supposed to have candy. Are you stupid? Where's my candy?" He didn't hear me. He didn't care. He was looking across the street now, not at me at all. The hot air in the car rose and lifted out the open window. It was unbearable.

"Hey, hey guys," Janie called from the bars. "Hey, what are you doing?"

She was sitting on top of the bars like on top of a cake with three tiers, her dark blond hair rumpled up in the back in a knot from rubbing it on the metal. Her one tartan hair-bow sat askew over her ear. Her naked

Barbie stood straight up beside her looking over her own right shoulder like her neck was broken, and upwards at the empty blue sky. I rubbed my hands on my shorts, but it made no difference. I looked at the car again, but Bobbie had me by the hand now, we were walking back to Janie so I couldn't say anything else even if I wanted to. Janie hadn't moved so we climbed up with her.

I hung upside down a good long time, chewing my Barbie's feet to bits, picturing Mrs. Turner, her high-spun hair and her beautiful, true face. The way she looked, kneeling to button our coats after class, her powdery skin, her eyes earnest, flicking back and forth as she told us about strangers and candy. "Don't take the candy, don't get into the cars," she breathed into my face, her palms flat on my flat chest. "Walk straight home." Then she lifted my braid and smoothed it, smiling. "Walk straight home, Emily. Nowhere else, please," knowing that I never did. I thought for a while how I'd get my revenge, how I'd tell my brother, how I'd tell Mrs. Turner. But somehow I just knew not to talk about it, since I'd walked to the car myself, since I was always walking somewhere I shouldn't. I felt somehow that I deserved it, the empty back seat, the stinging burn of his car bubbling up a long blister on my forearm. Above my knees, the sky darkened suddenly as it always did in the afternoons in August, and from two streets away I could hear my mother in her pearls and cocktail dress step out on the stoop to tell me that dinner was ready and I needed to come wash up.

Hush

"Hush," my father says, "hush, hush."

I go under again, *hush* the same sound as the water rushing into my ears, *hushhush*. Underwater I open my eyes, see his hand, a tentacle snaking towards me. Out of breath I surface, my mouth gaping like a fish's, my hair in my eyes. Water streams down. I can touch the bottom but not fast enough, his fingers around my wrist anyway, pulling me towards him, the water pushing against the hair on my naked torso, sliding like cloth. And so I pick my feet up and go under, watch my arm moving toward him until there's slack in his elbow. Then I pull hard twice and come free, sliding backwards through the flashes of sunlight moving in the water.

I watch him from underwater, the weight of the water like the flat of a hand on my head, I surface, gasp, go under again, my arms grabbing water behind me, hands cupping it for more purchase, pressing it forward, moving away, away. Everything in slow motion, the water impossible to be quick in. My hair floats out in front of my eyes, bouyant with air. And now he is under the water too, looking for me, his eyes wide open. There are bubbles in his eyelashes, his face is outlined in tiny bubbles. He wants my ankle and reaches for it, his palm up and open.

I push the water with my hands, they come out into the air and down, but I stay under. Bubbles sheet up everywhere. Lungs tight, I lie back under water and kick hard flat out at him, and when I come up to suck in air, he's there standing chest deep, one hand at his neck. He coughs shallow like a person with breadcrumbs in his throat.

"Hush," he says, coughing out the words. "I won't hurt you."

I'm sorry, I think. *I didn't mean to kick you.*

"Stay over there." I say it low like a man.

I am thirteen, and this is the last time he'll touch me. I mean to make it the last time. I have a new bikini, yellow with butterflies. I have breasts and hair. And he is swimming towards me, his head above water, his eyes locked on me, not losing me. He covers in seconds the five feet or so of distance I'd gained by kicking him. His pale arms under water look like glimpses of fish. I back up, but it's too slow that way, he swims more quickly. He hooks his hand around my bikini pants, the elastic stretching. It tugs at my groin.

"Come here," he says. He is standing in the water to his shoulders.

I can see the pool behind him now, where my mother lies in the sun and watches while my brothers horse around. Children boil in and out of the chlorinated water, tens of them. My father, my brothers, and I went first to the lake beside the pool; my brothers drifted back to the diving board, my mother dozing in the sun. I see her raise her hand and wave at us. The scarf she wears over her hair flips in the breeze. Her face is just over my father's shoulder. Her sunglasses cover her eyes completely.

"Come here," he says, and slides his hand around my waist until I can't move. My hair swirls in the water, a kind of seaweed, a kind of fish.

"It was an accident. I didn't mean to."

I say nothing.

"I swear it. It was an accident," he says.

"Let me go."

"It was an accident."

I say nothing.

"Jesus Christ. You're going to tell her, aren't you?"

"Let me go."

Calm. I fight for calm because I know that's how I'll get away. I want to kick him, hard, again. I want to punch his grim face right in. I want to hold him underwater until he dies.

He has me by the waist and I can't get anywhere. My arms, crossed over my chest, are pinned between us. I've arched my back so that only my forearms touch him; I am taut in a curve like the edge of something in a centrifuge. I look over his shoulder at my mother lying in the sun; she gleams with oil. She's turning pink, too fair for the light.

He drops me. Suddenly. I kick away a safe five feet, but now I can't touch bottom. I tread, my arms circling, circling, my hair sticks to my forehead, nets my cheeks. I watch him in case he's coming again. He stays where he is.

"Emily. Emily. Listen to me. Listen to me."

He had slid his hand over my breast, under my suit. He had moaned in my ear. Again. But today I am finished with him entirely.

I am listening.

"I didn't mean it. I swear I didn't."

I say nothing.

"I didn't mean it. Christ. Just don't tell your mother."

I say nothing at all but I make him go away, dissolve him in the bright specks of light glancing up from the ripples, focus my eyes past him so he becomes just another sunlit particle, another trick of light, another nothing in the water. Behind him, my older brother front-flips into the pool, an arc of spray articulating his curve. He shouts and my father answers, backing away from me, turning around to face them.

When he gets to the shore, the lake water runs off his body and back to where I am. But I don't care. I let my legs rise until I'm flat, afloat on the plane of the lake, my eyelashes pearled with water. I let the sky take everything over, then kick out to the lifeguard stand, where it's deep and cool, and I can dive.

Gator Bites

At the little cypress-sided gatehouse, the park ranger steps out to hand us a map and take our parking fee. She leans down into our window below the shadow of the canoe tied to our roof. Her eyes flick back and forth from me to my husband, Chuck.

"Boat launch is down the road some," she says, pointing vaguely behind her, "then to the right past the picnic tables. You can't miss it."

"Is there a beach there?" I ask, leaning forward from the passenger side so she can hear me. "Some place to go swimming?"

She shoves her hands in her pockets and squints into the trees for a long second or two.

"No," she says, at last, slowing the word up as if she's not certain. "No, there's no beach per se. I suppose you could just get in wherever you want. But," she adds, pursing her lips and looking in the window again, "most people find they'd rather not swim." In the line of cars behind us, a driver honks, his arm dangling out the window, his hand full of damp-looking bills. She waves at him as if he's being friendly, then hands us a final bit of paper and steps back to let us pass.

The two or three cars ahead of us crawl along in the dense shade. It's impossible to see the water; the verges of the road are crammed with yard-high palmettos, young cabbage palms, furry sapling slash pines. The oaks press close together, their limbs entwined and touching the ground here and there. They carry grape vine and Spanish moss inches thick everywhere, the tops of each branch a forest of resurrection fern, bright green from yesterday's afternoon storm. Moss brushes the bottom of the canoe, hangs up on the antenna. We park under trees the size of ships, their gray-black arms craning out and down, touching the sand. Mennonite children clamber on them, the boys in their blue pants, the girls in their little caps of stiffened gauze like miniature nurses. Their mothers stand in clumps under the awning of a cypress shack edged by six or seven empty picnic tables whose legs are half submerged in the ground. The women hold red-and-white paper cartons of gator bites, bits of batter-fried alligator tail, now and then passing a brown chunk to a child who ricochets near them. The men are off by themselves buying tickets to the tour boat, a huge, fan-driven double-decker, the fan as tall and broad as the trees, the shallow draft of the boat just enough for the weight of the passengers, enough to pass over a lake only four feet deep on average. The canoe launch is a ramp set into the water in a cove beside the air-boat dock. We untie the canoe, lift it off the top of the car, fill it with our things, equipment, wine, lunch in a basket. It's our second anniversary. The sky is clear and blue as it often is in Florida in March.

The water looks translucent and inviting, stained light brown with oak-tannin, cool and fresh when I put my hand in. I can see the grass on the bottom, the small fish moving their tails. I think about a swim, swing my end of the canoe out over the ramp, step in and wait for Chuck, who gets in the back. We paddle easily toward the flat expanse of lake that ends just before a horizon spiked with pines and brush. I dangle a foot over the side, my toes dribbling in and out of the water. About fifty yards in front of us floats a long piece of wood, a log or a big clump of cattails. I pull my foot into the boat, squint to see better, turn half around and say, "Honey, an alligator—look. Right there."

He looks, puts his hand over his eyes to shade them, frowns. "I don't think so. That's a branch."

"No," I say, pointing at the dark ridges in the water. "See, it's an alligator. Snout bump, eye bumps, tail bumps." I tick them off with my pointing finger—snout, eyes, tail. Its back appears, imagined, traced by my finger in midair. I've been away from Florida for years, forgotten alligators almost entirely, forgotten that I knew how to spot them at a distance, how they sun in the water like deadwood. This one looks about six feet long. To its left, more half-submerged alligators laze just under the surface. "See that? There's another one, and another one, and another one." My arm swings around, covers about forty-five degrees of a circle. Alligators are everywhere, like sticks in a flood.

"Cool," he says, standing up to get a better view. The canoe hardly rocks. "Just like on *National Geographic*."

"Better sit down," I say. "You don't want to fall in." I smile at him, a man who, as a boy, lay on the carpet in his spaceship-imprint footie-pajamas watching television shows full of tigers with their teeth clamped on some doomed antelope. He identifies with the tigers. He's excited that he can see first-hand a nature full of big, hungry animals like himself.

If he's not afraid, I tell myself, I'll be damned if I'm going to be. We paddle out of the cove and turn right, away from shore, following the curve of the lake's edge, which is furred with cattails for thirty feet or more until the marsh ends at the tree line. Alligators float by, rise, sink. A dozen maybe, maybe more. We go around them, watching the swirls where they flatten into brown stillness.

The sound comes from nothing. It starts like the burr of a stampede miles away, grows into a steady rustling and by the time we hear it clearly at last, it's big, wet, full of grunts and hissing. We stop paddling to listen better, focusing on the tall reeds about two hundred feet to our right. They part to frame an alligator the size of truck. Its feet are as big as my head, its mouth, open and huffing, is longer than my arm. Chuck says, "Fourteen feet. At least." He sounds awed. I remember a time when alligators were endangered and a fourteen-footer was a miracle that showed up on the news. I remember the first big one I saw, at the zoo; clinging to my mother, I watched it eat a frozen chicken, its skin pale and white, like mine. I think about the time a big one showed up in the bayou across the street, how we children stood in the muck and threw rocks at it while it glided on its way deeper into the mangroves. I remember the sound of the rocks plunking into the water and the animal's calm, silent swimming, its eyes just above the water, its tail just rippling the surface.

Chuck exhales audibly, puts his paddle in the water but doesn't move it. We watch as the huge alligator pushes itself out of the reeds, its underbelly flashing that shade of white that signals death, as slick and shiny as the satin in a coffin. It propels itself into the water with an audible whump, like the sound of a missile hitting the ground, and swims straight to us as if we'd called it. Suddenly the water smells swampy. I can taste it in my mouth. "Chuck." I say. "Chuck?" I see the gator clamp us by the middle, rip us apart like Moby Dick does the *Pequod*. I see this alligator open its mouth, snap our little boat in two, munch us for breakfast. "Damnit," I say. "Chuck."

The alligator doesn't change course. It gets close enough that I can see its eyes right above the waterline, twitching left and right in their orbits. I think: at night, those eyes glow red in the light. I read about that in school, that's how poachers know to shoot them. I think: if I were not in this boat, I'd be running. The animal is so big, moves so fast, it creates a wake that curls over and purls at itself, a wake deeper and wider than the one we can make in our thirteen-foot canoe, both of us paddling fast. The wavelets ripple out on both sides and back to the reeds, which slosh around.

I say, not turning around, "Chuck. Please. Can we go back to one of the picnic tables, okay? Now?"

"But why?" Chuck says. "Seriously, he's not even looking at us. He'll go underneath or veer or something." He's trying to be reassuring. "Come on. Don't worry." The alligator's still headed for us, his tail beating back and forth propelling him forward, his eyes like yellow-green marbles. I feel hypnotized. "Listen," Chuck says, "stop looking at it, okay? It's not going to hurt us. Let's go down there a little. Trust me," he says, pointing toward where the mouth of the river empties into the lake, "it'll be so nice down there." But we don't move right away, we can't, we're mesmerized. We sit watching until the alligator goes under a few feet from us, a submarine in a World War II movie, his eyes the conning tower, the last thing down. I try not to think about him down there, swimming beneath us, his fat tail whipping side to side.

When we start paddling again, we know we're moving out of the deeper water into the shallower, warmer water near the river because we can feel the pressure of the lake floor rising underneath us, how the boat gets lighter and more responsive. A heron lifts from a tree in front of us and heads back toward the boat ramp. We hear the air-boat behind us rev up and cut off and rev up again; otherwise we're almost entirely alone. Kingfishers, three or four of them, swoop and giggle; an enormous black bird that might be an eagle rides a thermal high up over the trees. The alligators proliferate, the lake brims with them, it's thickened like a stew with their basking bodies. At first we move slowly, mazing our way through. Sometimes we startle one, its tail whipping the surface of the water, making swirls and eddies. Snout bumps, eye bumps, tail bumps rise and fall uncountable as dust motes. But we get used to it after a few minutes, stop paying attention, pass right over them as if they are made of water. Chuck points at the trees, the birds, the sky. We chat, laugh, talk about anchoring and opening the wine.

And then we get stuck, grinding to a stop about five hundred feet offshore. I don't understand how we're stuck, but I imagine maybe the lake floor is uneven and we're on a ridge of silty bottom. I lean over, prod the water with my paddle. "What happened?"

"I don't know," Chuck says. "I think we're aground."

I push the paddle over the side, as deep as it'll go. I hit nothing but water. The ground isn't there at all, not where I'm sitting. I say, "I've got just water," but he doesn't hear me, because he tells me to push off the bottom. I put the paddle over the other side, lean over as far as I can. I say, "I've just got water, Chuck. Just water."

In the back, he presses with his paddle, but isn't getting anywhere either, so he starts rocking the keel left and right to free it. The lake makes little sloshing noises against the sides. I try to balance, concentrate on staying in the boat and not losing my oar. We still aren't free, so I lean over and dig. I say, "I still have water. What's—"

The boat stills suddenly. I turn around halfway to look at his face. He's holding the paddle and gripping the stabilizer bar with both hands, looking straight ahead like a train's coming and we're stalled on the tracks and ahead is where we really need to be, like now. There's no time for him to tell me to hang on.

The water erupts.

Chuck shouts from the back, "Paddle hard, hard on the left side! Turn us around, turn us around!" We're aground on a pile of alligators rolling wildly, writhing like the water's gone electric. They throw their limbs up and out of the water, slap them down again. I see a tail lift, turn over, slide under again. I see a leg, the toes clear and separated, the pads on the bottom of the feet. It comes up, goes under. The canoe rocks and slashes, water sloshes in cold on my wet thighs and over my head into my hair. As I set to working my oar, I see how, ahead of me, the cattails are lit in the wash of bright mid-morning sun, the olive-colored trees are dark against the clear sky. To my right, a man in a bass boat puts a line in the water, placid and calm as the weather. Bird watchers on a pier far down the lake point their binoculars elsewhere, their arms gesturing at the bright sky. It's beautiful, perfect even, so perfect, and I am utterly unperturbed, perfectly unafraid. I push my whole body against the water, concentrating every ounce of power into my back, my shoulders, my arms. I know I need to turn the canoe around, that I want the shoreline to swing over to my left. I want to stay in the canoe, for it to stay upright, afloat. I don't imagine dropping the paddle or tumbling out of the boat into the water. I don't imagine being pulled under, the cold water, the disorienting twirl in the alligator's grip, the drowning, the dying. I hold the oar and pull and imagine nothing at all but moving the boat right.

When I look over my shoulder, I see Chuck pushing the paddle at the alligators, trying to find something, anything not in motion to shove off of. "Keep paddling left, Emily." He's calling directions like a driving instructor, supernaturally calm. We have a task. I focus, I think, push, push, ignore the alligators, push push push. My shoulders burn, the paddle slips in my hands, spins slightly and I lose a stroke. I focus harder. I grip lower, my fingers are near the water with every pull, I lean left, lean left, lean left, the water snaps up over my wrists, but I am focused. Under me, bodies—jaws, tails, feet—go thump, scrree, thumpthump against the canoe. It sounds hollow, like knocking on a cheap door.

And then we are turning, the shoreline coming up now in front of me. The cattails are the same, toasting golden in the sun. The alligators, free of the canoe, roll over, push themselves up out of the water, fall on each other like dinner. Panicked now that there's no immediate reason to be, we skid toward the other end of the lake as if we're motorized, nearly airborne in straight flight away from the furor that doesn't subside until we can't hear it anymore. Chuck's paddling with such intensity that the front end planes up an inch or so even with me in it, and I lean over more to reach the water to keep us going fast. We aren't looking at the alligator bumps now. We want to mash them all, cleave them, hit them right between the eyes and chum them up with our keel. We move so fast that the airboat pilot stops as we cross paths, passengers leaning over the side to watch us blur like people possessed toward the nearby dam. All I can think of now is dying, drowning—dismemberment and blood everywhere. I say, "I want to go home now." I say, "I want a picnic table now."

"But," Chuck says, "we were going to—"

"I don't care. I don't care." I don't cry so much as wail.

The canoe hits the embankment moving so fast that it slides a few feet onto dry land before we know it. We wobble out, sit on the ground. Chuck presses up against me, puts an arm around my shoulder. He kisses my head. "Look," I say, "over there are picnic tables." He says, "But, sweetheart, we were going to eat on the water. We could eat on a table anywhere. It's our anniversary. It should be special." He'd spent the week planning this, the food in the basket, the canoe-trip, our being together outside where we loved it best. We would watch the birds and see what no one else could, something natural and unspoiled and beautiful. He'd worked it all out in his head—how we'd canoe, how we'd eat lunch, then lie back in the boat and watch the bright blue dragonflies cock their wings at us. I shift around on the sand, wipe my hands off on my shorts and smile at the two Black men fishing from the dam beside us, their long lines ending in red-and-white bobbers that sway in the current. The fan-boat is emptying onto the dock nearby, the Mennonites lining up at the shop for another round of fried alligator. I want some so intensely I salivate.

"Come on," he says, "let's just portage into the river. The alligators can't get over the dam, so it won't be scary. I promise." I can't explain why I believe him except that we are not dead, and he's smiling at me like nearly getting eaten by alligators is an adventure, an exciting adventure we're having together. He hops up, holds out his hand. I rise from the ground, wipe my nose on my t-shirt, and lift my end of the canoe. We portage to the deep water draining into the river behind the dam, get in and wave at the men, who wave back. They make a joke about an alligator, sixteen feet of it, that took off a man's toe the week before. They guffaw at the sight of my face, tear-streaky and terrified. I'm not laughing as we round into the river proper.

A chuffing full of wet air thrums rhythmically from the water. We look left together startled as if someone had dropped a book in a silent room. About thirty feet away on a hummock splotted with clumps of broken reeds and covered in mud mulched up with grass stands yet another alligator, this one bigger than any we'd seen all day, twenty feet long at least. He holds his mouth open a hands-breadth. It's slick and pale inside, whitish-gray porcelain draped like cloth into a tongue, gums, lips that scallop over his jawline. In between the jags of his teeth, a delicate bird hops and picks. The bird's head turns and turns, as if it hears something, it stabs now and then at a bit we can't see. The alligator huffs, grunts, shifts on his feet. The water we displace laps over his toes, slides away and ripples back toward us. We watch the little bird peck and chirp. We watch the alligator's eyes half-close. He huffs and sleeps as we slip away, not paddling much, not making much sound, downstream to where the alligators get smaller and smaller and finally are no longer than our forearms. We run the boat into the reeds, eat our lunch at last with the kingfishers, the eagles, a single heron perched in a tree.

A few days later, we tell my mother what happened as she sits in her Florida Room with the newspaper spread out over her brown Formica table. She sits with her back to the light outdoors, the bougainvillea blooming on the fence, the slash pine bending over the retention pond. She isn't actually reading the paper anymore. She gets a Kleenex from a box in the center of the table and dabs under her eyes. Her fingers, crooked with arthritis but manicured perfectly, blot at her underlids. Her pinkie finger shakes a little, like she's scolding. "You know better, Emily," she says. "Of all things. You grew up here. You know better. You can't blame him. He didn't know."

"Dear God," she says. "You could have died."

"I know," I say.

Chuck says, "But they were tiny when we finally stopped. It was a good picnic. We watched an eagle, ate some cheese. It was fine, Dody, just fine. Really."

"Of all things," she says.

"But we didn't die," I say.

Outside the automatic sprinklers come on and immediately it smells like egg-yolk or the cool center of hell. She shakes her head at no one, picks up the paper again. I sit on the other side of the table imagining she's looking for more stories to scare me with. I know she is. She learned this from my father who used to mail me Ann Landers columns on crushed motorcycles, the obituaries, gory descriptions of car wrecks. In the next weeks she'll send me articles describing a half-eaten corpse tucked into a crevice at Weeki Wachee like into the meat drawer, stashed for later; another one about a college girl, a late-night swimmer at a local trailer park, how they found her in the morning. An ear, some hair, part of a torso.

Later that night we take my mother to dinner at a seafood restaurant that serves fried gator tail. Chuck orders some and the bits come arranged on a bright green plate in a heap that steams. "Look," he says to my mother, "gator bites." He takes one from the pile, swipes it in horseradish sauce. "Umm," he says. "Gator. Food of the gods." We laugh as he eats it dramatically, chomping at it like revenge. Then my mother takes up a chunk too, a tough one she says, smiling a little as she chews.

For Panic, Say Five Things You See, She Says

1.   The Trunk is Old

The trunk lay on its side in my grandfather's Florida-hot attic. My father tipped it flat. I crossed my legs under me, addressed the two side-hasps, rusty with dirt, the center hasp a dead tongue, lolled down. With both hands I pushed the top up, lifted out an inner drawer, all striped like ticking. Underneath, a small woman lay with her arms stock straight to her sides. My father, busy with some boards, never saw her. She opened one eye. "Yello!" she said. The other eye winked open, two beads between black lashes. I knew she was kindly, so I took my braid out of my mouth. "Hey," I said. My father looked over his shoulder at me, frowned. "Hey," I whispered. "Gimme a hand," the woman shouted, reaching one out, "It's hoohot in here." When I touched her hand, the air rippled outwards like I'd dropped a stone in it. My father was gone. The attic had melted into nothing. I stood in an orange grove instead, the bees like sunshine humming by. "Katie!" someone shouted. I whipped around. "Katherine Belinda Soares, you put shoes on right now." And there I was barefoot, drowning in the jam-sweet scent of the afternoon, nowhere near home.

2.   Garter Stitches on an Afghan I Made

My mother could knit argyle socks, five or six bobbins in her lap. Her mother taught her, an Irish woman at five years old on the auld sod knitting mitten after mitten after sock after sock and still in her pinafores, The Great War still a coming conflagration. Instead of potato she said *bohdaydah*; she played cards like she couldn't lose. As "Marguerite," she jived with the jazz-boys in New York City, banging the keys, a cigarette stuck to her lip-rouge. She marcelled and bobbed her fine fair hair, her little blue eyes were canny jewels. Saturdays, she danced her diamante-studded garters on the bandstand. But she couldn't sing so they replaced her over poker, before she'd scraped in their week's pay and said, *See ya, suckers.* With that money, she went back to the mountains, bought a glass-eyed fox biting its own tail to wear, kept her hair marcelled but lost six years of her life on her marriage certificate. A businessman: they nodded at the butcher's, ended up in bed. He hit her afterwards only sometimes, when he was drunk and she was not too big with his babies. She practiced keeping low then, a small thing already, growing attenuated, legato. Her voice too, petering into a thready sweetness especially soft for the children.

3.   The Mended Dragon Vase

"BATTER UP," my brother cried. He hit the baseball across the living room, over the green plaid sofa, solid bounce, another against the ceiling, then down. I was there, I saw it. The crash sent him out the door. The vase on the table above me fell, fainting into pieces. Each one cried out coming down, what happened, what happened? The teal-painted dragon woke up in bits, his tail twitching over there, his one golden eye opening here, the hiss of steam off the whole thing like an engine come to rest. He flexed a paw, shot out a tender finger, ember hot, to touch my toe, a tiny flick of porcelain next to my nail. With careful attention, he lifted the sliver, licked it liquid, annealed it to a crisped and sharpened break behind his back. He hefted a second piece, mostly tail, liquefied and pressed and lo, the curvature of the vase appeared. I stared, wondering, the dragon's tail now lit like a lantern, my brother yelling from the yard, up a tree, falling out of it, up again like the earth needed pummeling by his body. The dragon pressed his finger to his newly assembled jaw. *Shhh*, he said, a little runnel of light between his teeth, *shhh*.

4.   The Thames above Henley Above an Urn of Barron-Dog's Ashes

They closed the college years ago, turned the whole place to junkshop, stacked stuff in corners like merchandise, cheap as dirt. I pick up someone's watercolor, autumn trees, turn it over: The Thames Above Henley, 1918, it says. *I'm dead*, the man beside me whispers. Half a face slack like a stroke, the other half taut, white, fair, one eye nodded closed, the other huge and empty except for the stars. I recognize Orion and his dog. The man puts a hand in his pants pocket, twists, points at the old blackboard, the ghost of the alphabet there. *I'm dead*, he says again, as if reading it. "This yours?" I ask, holding out the scrap of a river, a boat, some trees shedding summer into the water. *Dead*, he says, his lips unmoving. I try to read the name he's written in the corner, but it's illegible. I shake my head. I mourn now, the Thames water all washed by, the way Orion walks with his dog under the horizon, disappearing for whole seasons altogether. I pay cash for the picture, frame it, hang it just above my dog's bed. Dreaming, he sings to it in the night. I don't remember his voice, though I still can conjure the cool velvet of his ear between my fingers.

5.   The Green Faun

The hospice nurses tell her to go eat, she's been there for hours. We whisk her downtown. She takes her grandson by the elbow while I walk ahead with the map. She says, "Your grandfather would want you to have the statues." She says, loud so I can hear, "You should marry that girl." Back at her condo, her antique glass rings faintly with the traffic, the delicate bowls recollecting dust in silence, so many tongues and lips. They are Venetian, blown full of air. Like all glass, they settle so slowly no man notices, only wakes up decades later, the thick bottoms of his windowpanes distorting nature. From her corner, the bronze bacchante rises on one foot, each naked nail a delicate flick. She extends her arm, her other one around a child who tips toward the grapes she holds just out of reach, his face turned upwards with desire. The marble pedestal she stands on shifts when we open the door, the grandfather dead the minute we left him, our dinner uneaten. The grandmother with her bag and her dry eyes moves into the darkness of her house. Still finding the switches, she grabs the foot-tall bronze faun atop a globe atop dolphins, hands it behind her, blindly, nearly dropping it. "This is for your wife," she says, patting the wall. The light blooms. Chuck is looking over his glasses at me. The faun, held by its thighs, turns in his hands like a key.

Broody

"Broodiness [is] a hen's instinct to hatch [even infertile or imaginary] eggs. . . . Hens, like people, don't always react as you expect them to, and a persistent broody may continue no matter what you do." — *Storey's Guide to Raising Chickens*

"Honey?"

He is sitting at his desk, one phone at his ear, the other in his hand, his computer full of open chat windows, emails, other windows that flicker and ping. He mouths, *on the phone, the update collapsing.* Then raises an eyebrow.

"I'm going out to the farm, to look at the chickens."

He hits the mute button and sets down the headset and the cell. The landline's speakerphone buzzes, then chatters: "—the server room size is inadequate to the needs of the—"

"Look?"

"Look."

When we moved in almost ten years ago, we didn't redo the office. The boy whose bedroom it had been had dug holes with his shoes in the grass-green carpet under the built-in desk, cleated up a section of wall kicking something, who knows what. We found tennis ball marks on the walls inside the closet. The room suited Chuck this way. He added tack-holes in the ceiling when he hung blow-up planets for a video he took of his model *Enterprise* shooting past his balloon Mars. He stored a big box of sci-fi action figures in the closet, which he sometimes posed for Christmas videos featuring the Alien, Jean-Luc Picard, the baby Jesus, and one of our cats. He set up his telescope by the window, put a hummingbird feeder in the tree just outside, nestled a cat hammock on the sill. Over his workspace, he shelved novels by Ray Bradbury, Isaac Asimov, Arthur C. Clarke, Samuel R. Delany—the literature of his boyhood. At night, he watched sci-fi reruns on his laptop while I slept, then at breakfast re-enacted their plots for me, doing all the voices.

Today he sits in this boy-room trying to keep a data center working somewhere in Tennessee.

"Look. Look only," I repeat. I had promised: no chickens before we have a coop.

I meet his eye; he leans back in his chair. Voices on the speakerphone drone into the silence like hot, well-fed flies. Then a woman with a nasal twang pings into the conversation, mid-sentence: "—unless," she says, "unless we want the system to go down and all patient data to be dropped into nothingness and people to die." My husband spins around, punches a button, and falls into the ensuing babble, speaking rapidly and correctively into the phone. I was free to go—not to buy chickens, since I'd promised. Just to see them. I head out, purse in hand (total twenty dollars cash inside, I'm not getting chickens). I hit the garage door opener, walk past the stack of cat carriers, a perfectly-sized cardboard box, the bin of raggedy dog towels. I won't need them today. I'm just going to look. I decide to take the yard-work truck, the hauling-things-home truck, as a measure of my confidence. I grab the pull bar, lift myself up into the cab, program my GPS, and get on the road.

I leave my tidy, middle-class subdivision, take the bypass, a four-lane road that goes around the rigid square at the heart of our tiny town. I go north after a bit, then turn left into the trees, down a long rutted driveway dusted with gravel, past rows of pines a hundred feet tall or more, to where the house is. You'd expect maybe a house out of a Faulkner novel, maybe one with columns even (and to go around back to the coop where the help, a wrinkled old man, talks poultry to you as if you knew what he meant). Or maybe something like in a Walker Evans photograph—a dogtrot house, clean through the middle, a hound under a sagging porch balanced on stones, the dirt yard swept bare. The chickens with the hound under the house.

What you don't expect is a neat brick Cape Cod from a Michigan suburb, well designed and better maintained, with a green lawn that slopes down to a manmade beach on a private lake. You don't expect the children either—beefy, blonde girls, like kids fed on dairy in Wisconsin, only these two aren't sweet and silent and slow like the cows. They're more like the ducks and chickens they raise, one eye on you, tilted, quick, judging. The girls hold kittens a few weeks old who pour over the tops of their hands and skitter across the ground and over my feet, darting into a hiding place under an outbuilding. The children say nothing to me about the kittens or why I'm there. Their mother wants them to root the mama-kitty out of the garage so she can close the door, so they're lifting things, skirting the tractor, making squidgy noises about spiders. They stop near the lawnmower. "She's under there," they say, almost simultaneously, like a chorus. The smaller girl pushes a strand of blonde hair behind her ear. She stands on one foot watching her mother, who tells them just to leave the door open and never mind. Then she cocks her head left. "You want to see the flock, yes?" Yes.

We pass through a cattle gate in a post-and-wire fence that encloses maybe an acre, maybe more, of trash trees, pines, brush, and birds. Standing just inside near a bucket of feed and vegetables, she points out the ducks with pom-pom heads. "They're rare," she tells me. "Best profit margin by a long shot." They paddle in children's plastic wading pools, feet tickling images of fish and Elmo, quacking furiously at nothing in particular. Chickens bunch and run all around us, hundreds of them, feathers the color of steel or copper, brown, dingy-white, black-green, orange, their combs fire-red. One bird's lipstick-colored wattles hang to his belly and swing when he turns his head; they look like slack, sunburned testicles. The flocks move under the trees like schools of fish, the lead birds in a phalanx. It is remarkably quiet aside from the quacking.

Twenty or so chickens sprint toward us, their yellow and white legs pumping up a cloud of dust, the lead rooster's loose-skinned face quivering and shaking. The birds pool around our feet, chuckling warmly as if to comfort us. She picks one up, a light Sussex hen with a horrible, mutilated back, who looks like she's been partly prepared for roasting but left alive. Her head darts left, right.

"Shredded by a rooster," she says to me. "This one'll need an apron." She chucks the hen under the chin in a familiar way.

We walk over to a stack of wire pens, and she deposits the hen in one of them. In three others, chickens lie quietly on nests. Two of them wear what look like canvas tank-tops with the fronts missing, their wings drawn through adjustable straps. "Recovering from mating," she says. "See that?" I look at a pen just beside these, on the ground and much larger. "Coronation Sussex. He needs more babies, so I've penned him with some of his hens."

"Beautiful," I say, and he is: large as a small turkey, he's the color of snow in the dusk, with a velvety moss-gray collar and a fountain of stony-gray tailfeathers. His legs are an absolute white, their spurs long and sharp like ivory daggers. In the yard, a rooster crows, and then another. The rooster in his pen struts, lifting and lowering his feet like he's testing the ground. I hold my breath. He puts his head back, closes his eyes and crows so loudly the titmice in the tree over us startle into air. I step back, then forward. I want him to do it again.

"Are they always that loud?"

"He's showing off," she laughs.

In the pen, the hens crowd a corner, thinking she's come to feed them, trying to avoid the rooster as he puffs up and shakes out his feathers. They follow us along the fence as we pass them, tuck-tucking softly, hopefully.

She scoops up a black chicken from the crowd still milling at her feet, moves her into a patch of light. She shines like she's been oiled, her yellow feet kicking. Then I notice she's actually green, British racing green, the deep, shadowy felt-green that looks black but isn't. I want to hold her. Her yellow eyes have a fringe of lashes. Her comb is the pink of lipstick for girls. She weighs nothing as she settles into the crook of my elbow.

"I expect you'll want chicks, right?"

And I find that I do.

I put the bird down, and we go to the hatchery in her garage, a small room full of chicks in big plastic tubs. Under the heat lamps, the babies peep and scuffle and bump, raise up on tiptoes and flap their nubbins of nearly-wings. None is white; some are brown, some black, some yellow, the color of bread-crust. Some have brown stripes or blotches of lighter or darker fuzz. Their eyes are button-black dots in their bird faces. Looking down at them, I discover a new kind of greed. I want to take them all.

But I can't. I can't take any, in fact. Birds mean responsibility, commitment, caring for a living thing for years. I can't just scarf them up like a forbidden candy bar in the bathroom when I get home, then brush my teeth and deal with the guilt. I can't take any.

"Hmmm," I say. She picks one up, hatched a few days ago. A little Wyandotte, yellow and brown. I do quick math: two isn't enough. Eight? Five? I promised to get none. We don't have a coop. The chickens peep into the hot silence like cheap alarms.

"How about three? I need three girls," I say, "and a box. A Sussex, and a Wyandotte, a-ah, a Marans. Will they be okay in a box for the rest of the day? We—um, we don't have a coop."

"Sure, and anyway they only need a bin at this point. Can't be cooped until they get bigger and start getting feathers. So you're fine taking these with you."

I look down at the chicks, about twenty-five of them in the bin. They smell like sweet corn and hot barn.

She smiles, pulls down a cardboard box. "I expect you know about food and watering? And heat?" I nod. She pulls a baby from the bin, yellow like chicks at Easter, and puts it in the box. The Sussex. Then a brown one with little flecks on its wings. Wyandotte. She cheeps at the buttery-colored one, snuggles against it. Their claws scrabble on the cardboard. The last, black fluff with a yellow rump, the Marans. She closes the box, hands it over, takes my ten-dollar bill, says thank you as she escorts me out.

And there I find myself, promises shredded to confetti, on the road home with three tiny chicks chattering away in a flat box in the backseat of the truck. *Peep*, they say, over and over, sweet and high. Their voices don't stop my crying at the stoplight, and the next one, in a kind of desperate shame. *Peep peep*, they say, their fuzzy heads filled with nothing. I want to stop and take them out, just to hold them, look at them. I'm imagining what owning chickens will be like, thinking about whether they'll be hard to raise, whether they'll be like cats, whether laying eggs hurts them.

I'm also wondering what'll happen when I tell. I wonder if I have to tell, ever. If I can hide them in the garage until one day we're just standing at the window and I've let them out, and he says, *Are those chickens?* And I say: *Yes, they're our chickens, aren't they wonderful?* and then we hug while we watch them peck in the yard.

And I think about how the next time I promise something I'll be thinking: *Oh, the chicks, I lied, I couldn't help myself, I never can.* This makes me cry harder.

I try deep, cleansing breaths, the ones I learned in yoga years ago, until I get light-headed, which makes me worry that I'll crash the car and kill the chickens, so I stop. I keep driving, driving carefully like I have a new infant in the back rolling around in a box on the upholstery. The corners I take slow and wide. I get home, leave the babies in the truck. "Shh," I say. "I'll just be a minute."

I am standing at his office door. I may still be crying. He is not on the telephone for the moment, though he's still wearing his headset and the computer pings and pings.

"You got chickens, didn't you."

Not a question. "They're in the car."

"How many?"

"Just a couple." I pause. "Three, actually. A Sussex, a Wyandotte, and something else. A Marans."

He swivels in his chair. Behind him the computer refreshes his email and an IM pops on top with a tweety ping. He turns, answers it, turns back. "You'd better show me."

I open the box on the backseat, the chicks peeping their hearts out inside.

"They need a bin and a heat lamp," I say.

"And food, and water. And stuff to eat out of." He picks up the Marans, runs a forefinger down her back to quiet her. "Tractor Supply Store. Go on." He takes the box from me, waves me out of the driveway.

I buy a heat lamp, chick crumbles, a bright red feeder—about twenty dollars of supplies (the chicks were ten dollars, all three)—doing math in my head for comfort. How many cartons of eggs is the bag of crumble? How many for the feeder? How to calculate for the way they'll eat their weight in bugs, for the savings in tick bites and black widow stings, of the roses eaten through with Japanese beetles? What are the savings in hassle? In chemicals? In trips to the vet and the doctor? Is this an argument? Will I need to argue to keep them?

But there's no need, there never is. He makes room for them, like everything I bring home—goldfish, turtles, kittens, stray dogs, hungry students. When I get home, he puts together pine shavings and a dish of water in a big blue bin in my office, rigs the heat lamp so it dangles from the fan. Then tucks a handful of grass into a corner, green and hot with Spring, to help them know about the backyard. For the smell and the taste of it. "Grass?" I ask. "Do they even eat grass?" This is how much I don't know, this is my relief in his acceptance of my soft heart, of the taking-in I do, of my enthusiasm for what I don't know. I get the box from the garage, set it down on my desk, and pick up the black one with its butterball of a butt. Its feet press against my palm, its beak opens and closes.

I hold it out and say, "Let's call this one Jadzia, okay? Like that character from *Star Trek* you love."

"*Deep Space Nine*."

"Whatever. Jesus, I'm sorry. *Deep Space Nine*."

He reaches out and lifts her foot with his finger. She curls her toes around it like a baby learning to roost.

"Anyway, Jadzia? Yes? It's okay?"

"Yes, it's okay."

I set the chick in his hands, its peeping quick as panting, where it pushes and scrambles until he sets it by a bowl full of rocks and water beside its two nest-mates. They all drink just like bobbing robins, down and up on the pivot of their hips, then discover the grass as if they were stumbling on a brand-new universe.

Ducking

Hand halfway to the cafeteria door, I'm listening this morning to the noise off the small, dirty lake with its carillon like a fist rising straight out of the water. I'm thinking: the swans must be at it again.

The half-dozen or so black swans specifically, with Christmas-red beaks, and sleek, slatey feathers. They're beautiful, serene as cats, smooth as courtesans, but bitter and angry and not to be trusted. From our dorm rooms on weekends we watch them chase people picnicking on tartan blankets, the toddlers with bread in their hands, the alumnae mothers with tidy hair tied in scarves. The children stand near the water tossing crusts to a mixed bunch of ducks and swans, but when the food is gone, the swans nip whatever they can catch. The women grab their children, turn their own shoulders to the birds who pinch a bit of skirt, a t-shirt tail, a little chunk of leg. College boys run over to help, taking off their shirts in one overhand sweep and flapping them at the birds. The women thank the boys who are putting on their shirts, who will watch the women leave in that way that boys do.

This morning the swans are making noise too early, far too early for picnickers, so I drift from the cafeteria door over a few feet of short grass just beginning to green up. It's not the swans, who waddle around as silent as trees. But about ten feet out into the water, the lake boils around a single duck, a little brown bird with black-button eyes. She splashes, quacks, flaps her wings to fly or swim but just beats the water into the air. She goes nowhere but under, coughing and quacking and fighting. Then a second duck bobs up, a different duck, large and sleek, his wings and feet kicking the water into turmoil. The two birds writhe and struggle, the larger one on top using its bill like a ball-peen hammer, pounding the little duck's nape. Like a blacksmith. Like a wind-up toy. They go under. The one on top quacks, slips, submerges. The smaller one swims for it, but the other bird is faster, catches her, stands on her back, pounds the back of her head until I can see feathers come out. The little duck goes under and comes up and goes under and swims frantically for somewhere she won't drown. She calls out and calls out, but this only brings more big ducks.

"They're going to kill her," I say out loud, though no one's there. I shout, "Hey, cut that out!" The ducks pretend I don't matter. The little one, too—she's swimming toward the center of the lake just as if she wants to die. But I imagine her quacking means she doesn't, that the back of her bloody head says she doesn't, that the way she keeps bobbing to the surface means that if someone would help her, she would choose to live.

I think: *I could save her*. I could drive her to the vet, get her head stitched up, see her warm and safe. As I stand there watching her fight, I imagine for her a life of domestic safety, a box with soft lining and regular duck-chow meals, no children with stale bread to have to be grateful for, no wooden drakes and gunshots and falling out of flight, nothing but safety from here to a natural grave. I could save her.

I quickstep toward the lake, not quite running. The swans, alarmed, writhe their necks and hiss, but I swat them away, hiss right back at them, veer around them through the wide-eyed Muscovies and mallards who quack in surprise. I charge right over the dirty fringe of grass and muck and trash straight into the lake.

It's just past winter. The water sinks into my shoes like a fall of pebbles, fills up my socks, grabs my calves and thighs and sex and then, with a tentative tongue, laps my navel. I say nothing at all, just stand there, big and strange. Me upright like a pillar in the lake, that has to mean something. Then I clap and shout to catch the ducks' attention. They stop, uncomprehending, look over their backs at me, at the ripples I send toward them as a message that I will not tolerate any more of this. "Leave her the hell alone," I say, waving my arms. I want something to throw at them. "You leave her alone."

While I shout, the ducks all sit in the water, letting it buoy them to the surface, their feet turning them this way and that on the pivot of their hindquarters. Then, like BBs dropped on a smooth surface, they scatter. Even the little one goes, her black eyes wary. She quacks her alarm, watches me over her bleeding shoulder, the feathers sodden and broken. I stand up to my waist in the filthy lake, working on being satisfied that at least she won't die. That she will be safe as long as I stay there, watching.

I don't know much about ducks, just that my father—a man's man who likes to hunt when he's not sitting behind a desk in his Armani suit—goes to Texas every once in a while to shoot them. He brings coolers of dead fowl home in checked baggage for my mother to clean, cook, and serve.

She hates these ducks, her hands in their cold, wet feathers, her hands in their insides pulling out pink and black and gray things, goop to throw away, wads of yellow fat slick as eyeballs. She works the bodies top and bottom, pulling, cleaning, cutting. Her wedding ring flashes in the light from the window as she chops and saws until only the meat is left. She feels through it all for the tiny pebbles of birdshot, lifting them out with her nails or pinched between her finger and thumb. I know just how a stray shot that my mother hasn't found strikes against a molar when I bite down, tastes of metal, hard and inedible. How it pings into the plate like a BB from my brother's pump rifle—the same brother who got duck pox one year by touching the birds at a pond near our house, petting them slick down their sinuous necks, fingering the deformities of skin on their faces. We knew not to, of course, but he did anyway. Mornings, our mothers would sit on picnic benches holding plastic bags of bread and talking to each other, watching us through their sunglasses to make sure we didn't drown. All the children in our city did as we did, flocks of them at the water's edge with us, holding crusts out to the fat ducks who were tame enough to like to be touched, rubbing up against our legs like dogs so we could run our fingers through their back feathers down to their skin. *Dirty, dirty*, our mothers would say, wiping us all over with damp towels, pulling out the Mercurochrome for the nips the birds gave us, our fingers pinched and painted red.

But the lake is cold and dark with muck and my lower body begins to numb. I tuck my hands into my armpits, watch the poor little duck swimming away for another moment, then turn around and wade out, the water running back through the dirt and grass into the lake. Each shoe weighs like an anvil. I sit and take them off, then each sock, wring out the bottom of my jeans, wipe my hands on the grass, then on my sweater. The swans pace warily nearby. One flaps his wings and I see where they've cut away his flight feathers in a grotesque notch.

Warmer than the air, the water clouds off me in steam, like under my clothes I've caught flame. The bones rattling in the cold are my teeth. I pick up my shoes and socks, dead grass clinging to them, my bare feet without feeling now, stone-blue and just as heavy. A friend from the hall arrives with a towel. "The duck," I say to her, to Jenny, "she was—"

"I know," she says. "We were watching."

Her pearls have a sapphire clasp that's turned around to the front, a wish she'll have to make later. She's painted her lips naked pink to match each perfect oval fingernail. She folds the towel gently over my shoulders as if I were a million years old, senile and feeble and maybe never smart to begin with. She takes my muddy arm, helps me up, and we slosh up the stairs together. My jeans drip and reek.

"The duck," I say again, "she was dying. I couldn't save her."

"Yes. I'm so sorry. We saw." She rubs the towel on my back in small circles, a kind of comfort.

When we get to my room, she gives me another towel, takes my wet clothes when I hand them out of the shower to her and wrings them out in the sink, drops them in a plastic bag for taking to the laundry. The bathroom smells like my skin, my clothes, there is dirt in my underwear and between my toes, clayey and cold and molding itself to my body. It drops off in clumps, melts into the drain and disappears like it never was.

Jenny closes the door to let me finish, but when I'm dry and dressed again she says, "So." And I say, "Make a wish," and turn her sapphire to the back. "It never stays there," she tells me, her brown eyes the color of leaves in winter. She looks into my face like she wants to see something that isn't there, then raises her hand to her neck, checks the necklace. She keeps the hand there, fingers patting softly against the pastel blue of her sweater-set. The tiny buttons are mother-of-pearl pierced with two needle-fine holes.

"So," she begins again, then sits on my roommate's bed, tucks her feet under her, leans forward earnestly. Her elbows balance on her knees. I sit on my bed, on a comforter covered in print images of the beach, each peach seashell a whorl of pinks cradled in golden sand. I'm cold still and my hair's wet, so I pull the corners up around me like a closing flower. Jenny leans over and picks up my roommate's only stuffed animal, a baby-sized teddy bear. She hugs it across her chest, its brown, pokey legs splayed out over and under her arm.

"Ducks," she begins. "Well. You . . . you've never been on a farm?"

"No, Florida. Beach. Remember?"

"No. Of course not. Okay, so ducks. They're—well, they're—you know. Ducks."

She shrugs. Her fingers fiddle with the bear's ear. I huddle down a little further into my comforter.

"Ducks are ducks," I say.

"Okay, so, you, um, you know all about—"

I sit, staring at her face. She's not looking at mine. She's watching her hands and the bear and she's obviously trying hard to make me understand something.

"You know, don't you, about babies?"

"Babies?"

"Yeah, babies," she says. "Babies from eggs and stuff."

"Jesus, yes, Jenny. Tell me you're not going to give me the talk."

"Well, I thought maybe it would be a good idea. Since, you know—" She gestures vaguely in the direction of the lake. Then she blushes bright red.

"Yes, I know where babies come from. What has this got to do with what was happening to that duck? It was drowning, Jenny. They were bashing her head in." I start shivering again. "They're going to kill her, I know it."

"Ducks are different."

"Different."

"Well, not all that different from some people but not, you know, us maybe."

"Us? What are you talking about?"

"No one's getting hurt, Emily. They like it like that."

"She was bleeding, Jen. And drowning. And screaming. She did not like being beaten on the head. No one likes being beaten on the head until they bleed. No one."

Jenny sighed. "Maybe not us. Maybe some people we know, though. Maybe, you know, people who like to get hurt sometimes, with someone they love. The duck will live, I promise you." She puts her hand on the place where my arm is tucked in the comforter, presses down, then turns and replaces the bear on the pillows. "It's just—Spring, you know? They're making ducklings. It's just Spring." She nods at herself, like that's what she needed to say, like now I would understand. "Breakfast now? Yes?"

From below the window, voices rise and fall like marching feet, someone laughs and another person stumbles. A book bag drops, rasps on the pavement, is shouldered again. Someone says, *I think it might rain. Do you think it'll rain? I think it will.*

Jenny's getting her keys, smoothing out her pants. The part in her hair is startling white, like a scar, like a raw place before it begins to bleed. I could only stare and think how I had no idea, saw nothing the way it was, knew nothing about the way things are. I didn't know that the little brown duck wasn't dying, wouldn't die, would nest and lay eggs and raise ducklings, and do it all over again come next Spring. That she wanted it, she enjoyed the bloodied head and near drowning. That it was the cost of motherhood and she didn't know anything else: this is how ducklings have been made since forever, since the duck or the egg began. By now they were at it again, in fact. I imagined her down in the muck, the bloody feathers, the riot and violence and calling out. She didn't need saving any more than I did, couldn't be saved, shouldn't be saved, didn't want saving. Jenny's holding the door, and I get my umbrella from the stand. My laundry will wait for after lunch, I think, though the room stinks of it already.

Real Parents

I am fifteen. Their house is in our backyard, kitty-corner from our grapefruit trees. The parents call, ask me to come babysit their little blond boy at seven that night. I show up. They say, "Rick needs spanking sometimes. Will you do that for us?" I nod. I ask, "What do you mean, spanked?" They say, "Paddled soundly, you know, with your hand." I nod again. That night the child misbehaves, I push him onto the bed and aim a ridiculous slap at his behind. He yells. I stop. He thrashes dramatically around in the bed, gets up, screams, runs in circles, throws himself back on the mattress. I trundle him under the covers and sit on him (he's seven or eight years old). He struggles, cries, hates me, struggles, hits me. I sit, I say soothing things, tell him a story. He falls asleep, finally. The next day the parents call me, the father on the phone, out of the blue, "Do you think it's okay that Rick dresses in girl's clothes? Do you think he's queer?" I'm fifteen. I say, "I think he's probably fine but doesn't like being spanked." The father hangs up. I brood on this, on and off, for the next thirty-two years.

For instance: my father and I are standing in the dark in the yard. I have just learned that if you find and follow the North Star, you will always head north. My father has never heard of this. I look up and point at the sky. I say, "There's the Big Dipper, there's the North Star. That way is north." My father looks down at me. He doesn't look at the sky at all. He says, "That's not true. You can't trust a star." I say, "The teacher said it was so. Why would he lie?" My father says, "You're so gullible. I don't believe it. Besides, what do they do south of the equator?" I ponder the question. I don't have an answer. I'm eleven years old.

We have the same conversation when I'm fourteen about nouns in German, a language his parents abandoned during World War I, but about which he believes (by virtue of his blood) he knows more than I do, since he's German and I'm not. He has decided to take German classes. He knows a word or two from war films, which he uses on the dog because yelling in German is more yell-y. I say, "You know, German nouns decline and have gender." His blue eyes bore into me. He is deciding if he knows what those words mean. He says, "No, they don't." I say, "I've read about this, they do." He says, "You don't know anything about German. I know. My parents were German. You're not German at all. What do you know?" We leave it at that.

On the other hand, here we are, a sunny day in Spring and I have driven up to see my brother and sister-in-law, my tiny blond nephew just two or three years old. He's sulky, playing basketball in the driveway. He throws one wide, runs after it, trips and scrapes his knees. My sister-in-law, standing in the garage talking with me, notices but waits for him to come to her. When he does, mad and crying, she says, "You're just having a bad day, aren't you?" She smooths his hair, kisses his knee. He runs off to play again. I think, "That's all it really is, just a bad day and not a catastrophe."

It's my dissertation year, and I'm balled in a heap in my therapist's office, on the sofa, grieving. My first marriage ending, my career imploding (stalled then by misfortune and mismanagement), my father's dying suddenly, my home lost in the divorce, all the losses of two years of blow after blow. She lets me cry. She lets me talk. I say, "I want the hurt to stop. I want not to care." She says, at last, "This has been so difficult, this time. Hurting is normal. You are normal. Think about it: who would you be if you weren't sad about your divorce? Who would you be if losing your job didn't matter, if you felt nothing about the loss of your home, your work, your family? Tell me, would you want to be that person?" She is rearranging the world so it makes sense, so I can see and understand. She's probably said this to me several times before, but on this day, I hear it. I hear it so well, in fact, that when students come sobbing into my office, their arms and their lives full of every kind of loss, I tell them what she tells me, "Who would you be, if you could lose so much and feel nothing? You have to feel. Otherwise, what are you? Do you want to be that person?"

The neighbor in a tiny house down the street has a number tattooed on her forearm. I don't know what it means until after she dies and I'm far away, far older. I am child in the '70s: she is the only woman I know with my name—Emily. Her last name, Felgenhauer, is German, like mine. I spend most of my childhood afternoons in her parlor and kitchen, alone or with Bobbie Jean, my best friend. Mrs. Felgenhauer is a little woman, her hair is still dark, her rings are loose on large-knuckled fingers that produce what we, at five and six and seven years old, believe is the most beautiful music. She gives us lemonade, sits us on her chairs, and plays waltzes on the piano for us. After a few of these and some impromptu dancing, we head to the kitchen where something, always something our parents would never fix, is waiting to be eaten: strudel, fried chicken liver, caviar, matzo ball soup, hard boiled eggs deep fried in a batter shell—so much I can't remember. One day I watch as she prepares an apple pie and puts it in the oven. She plays the piano for me, teaches me "Heart and Soul" or something else easy as we wait, and when the pie is done, she cuts me a big slice. "Sour cream?" she says, as if I know what that is. I make a face. "Oh," she says, "you just don't like the word *sour*. I promise, you'll love this." She hugs me and laughs, and I laugh too. I think about it for a minute, make her promise it isn't sour, then agree, as a good sport, that I'll have some, thank you. I remember my first taste of sour cream, how she uses what she knows about me to get me to try it, how she opens up a whole world for me in her kitchen, in her living room.

Much later, working in Wisconsin, I show up at a friend's house with a gift for her little girl. My friend has taught her daughter sign language. The present has a big red bow tied around it chunky enough that she can open it herself. My friend shows her daughter the present, and the daughter, with big eyes, signs, *Star, star, star*. Susan and I are confused. Star? What star? The child, frustrated, signs more furiously, looking anxiously into her mother's face: *starstarstarstar*. Susan points to the ceiling, the child points to the present: *starstarstarstar*. Suddenly we understand: the bow looks to the baby like a star. Instead of correcting her, Susan tells her that it does look like a star indeed, tells her that she's clever, and we put the present aside for a minute to draw stars on paper for me to take home. *Starstarstarstar*. It doesn't matter it's really a bow if she imagines stars when she sees it. Another friend in Wisconsin serves her four-year-old son rotini. He takes two pieces off the plate, rearranges them on a napkin so as not to mess up the table. He eats and simultaneously narrates the story of worms on an adventure with the two napkin-rotini. His mother helps him with plot—"When they reached the river, what did they do?"—and asks him questions about the intersection of story and fact—"When they get to the edge of the napkin, are they frightened?" When he's done eating, they go dig in the garden, find worm-friends for the rotini, leave the pasta in the grass so they can have lives uncircumscribed by what they really are, or the square of a napkin. The child is not confused; rotini is food—and he ate his lunch with traveling friends, in hope and a kind of freedom.

Soon after we move to Florida in the 1960s, my mother takes my brothers and me over to St. Cecilia's to get us signed up for catechism. There's a form, she enters RC when it comes to religion. I need to know what RC stands for. She says, "Roman Catholic, that's what we are." I know not to ask any more questions, since her face has that look. She turns the form in, sits us in a row on hard wood chairs. My legs dangle. She whispers to the nun, who looks over at us, then up into my mother's face, then takes my mother in the back by her arm. This is how I know that I am not my mother's real daughter: she has to tell people in secret who I am. Years later, when my paternal grandparents move to Florida, I understand that I am not real because I am adopted. That my parents aren't my real parents, aren't real parents at all, though I am their daughter. They claim me in public. I behave like a Hipchen, but at home I am not a Hipchen (my wild dark hair, my unruly eyebrows, my unruly body). Not German, not like them, but sole and unbelonging.

On the day my other mother calls, I feel unreal, above and out of myself, surprised and joyful and out of my mind. I feel even more unreal on the day I meet her and my father, the man she married shortly after my relinquishment to the nuns at the orphanage thirty-five years ago. My friends say, "You are meeting your real parents, how does it feel to meet your real parents?" My mother in Florida says, "I am so happy for you, your real parents at last." When I meet my birth parents, they are there (real enough), but not present (my mother looks down, away, elsewhere; my father walks behind us, silent). To me, they are strangers who look like me, parents for sure (how else to explain what we are to each other?) without having parented me. We pose for a photograph, which looks even less real when I get it back from the printer. I think, "Did I ever look like that? Was I there?"

When as a young woman I answer the phone at my mother's house, her friends say, "Martha! What are you doing?" I explain that I'm Emily, her daughter. They say, "You sound so much like her, it's hard to know it's you and not her." I have not inherited her voice. How do I sound like her?

When my father answers the phone, he talks like a movie version of a Long Islander, like he has a dialect coach, but of course he doesn't. His accent is real, lived, all *cwafee* and *Lwon Guylind*. I could never be mistaken for him on the phone, for the man whose body I come from, whom I most resemble in body.

When I visit her, I hear my little sister laughing for the first time from the other side of the house. We're close to the same age, in our thirties. We've only just met. I think, *That's how I laugh. Exactly.*

My older brother, the one I grew up with, blue-eyed, hard-bodied, is direct and emphatic, no chit-chat, no dicking around, cut and dried and get it done. That's how I am, exactly.

I think how I'm adopted, how I was relinquished, moving from one person—my mother—to another—my mother. How in less than a week I was born and abandoned and three months later, taken up again. Neither of my mothers feels entirely like my mother, entirely real. To me, to each other, to themselves.

But I want them to feel real; I want to feel real myself; I want to feel the reality of all my family. I want to stop thinking "real," entirely, as if you could birth or raise a child and not be real.

Underwater

Every morning, Anna, who will become my mother but not yet, finds the little string with its tiny silver bell at the bottom and pulls the light on. Her face appears in the mirrored cabinet, her hand opening the door, taking out the Pepsodent, her toothbrush. She slicks down her hair with her hands, curls up the ends with her fingers dipped in setting lotion. Her face is fuller than she remembers. The bath runs, she puts a hand in the water, warms it some. She wears baby-doll pajamas. She strips the bottom, the elastic cut and held with a pin now, her top loose enough for her breasts, the spattering of roses over the whole, less like freckles than the careful pink ending of a thousand sentences. She lifts her long, lovely seventeen-year-old arms, her clothes drop down. She says nothing. It is morning, her sister is waking up. The woman steps into the water, settles into it, her big belly floating like a buoy. She whispers, "Wake up, Joanna." In my own ocean, I rise and flex, through her skin my one fist pushing the bath water into ripples.

***

A few months later, Anna paces the hall at the Home, listening to babies wailing in the distance, women wailing. Her water has not yet broken. She knows that when it breaks, her baby will leave her, and she will have to give it to the nuns and walk away. As she paces, one hand on her stomach, one on the wall, she says to me: "Finger in the dam, Joanna, gather up the waters." So I make a ball of myself, imagine myself the tiniest dot, smaller than a period. I am a snail shell, a heavy bead on the bottom of this ocean. Later, born, I will become a fish drowning in air while my mother empties onto the floor of the delivery room. She remembers the doctors calling for help, their hands pressing hard where I left her, another hand sewing, another hand taking away the packing, pressing more. Thirty years later, she tells me I cried to throw the walls all down, swinging there upside down in the cold light, fire-engine red, pocked and slick-white.

***

ANIMAL HUSBANDRY

In my new family, I am bathing, pressing my fat belly against the plastic daisies stuck to the bottom of the tub. The warm water makes islands of my back, of my shoulders pushing up, my head an immense and heavy bloom rising on a short, unstable neck. My other mother wets a washcloth, rubs a restless pudgy foot. I look over my shoulder and shiver dramatically, my eyes giant, velvety, heavy-fringed, the color of whiskey. I shiver again, press an arm down, fold the other accidently, and roll over flat on my back. She gasps, thumbs her lit cigarette into the tray on the back of the toilet: "You rolled over," she says, patting her hands together. The water washes into my ears, my inky curls unwinding. I hear my heartbeat now, the whispering too, sighs and voices and song. I blink, listening hard, about to understand absolutely everything. She lifts me. Water drops dangle from my fingers and toes, pinging back into the bathtub. The towel is cool, rough, so I cry and pound my head on her shoulder. She imagines a nap, and not absolute submersion, will calm me.

***

I rise with the sun out of the ocean off the Cape, snap on my suit with all its stiff ruffles, open the door without squeaking it. The sand buckles under even my little weight. My footprints trail behind me. At the wash, the waves rush at me rushing them; then to my waist in the water, a cold that touches and bounces and careens, full of tiny fish, salt crystals, granulated shells. It pushes and bounds, my narrow chest a nothing, a keel. The sea presses itself against me. I kneel into it, open my eyes underwater in the chatter and clutter. I lift my legs in the cold, so creamy and thick that I rise in it, my legs two parentheses, my arms and fingers spread to ride the surf back. I lie in the water, the stars still salting the western sky, the dawn full of its own energy. Soon, my mother calls with her Kools and her coffee from the door. I pick up a fistful of sand to show her. I run toward her voice, shells and seaweed and salt sugaring me. "You can't swim alone," she says. "Children drown all the time." She tucks a sticky curl behind my ear as we wait for the light.

***

At the edge of the shell-fall, the water darkens. The bottom is invisible, like the sharks and skates. Little fish are silver dashes in the dim. Water passes through my braid, over my shoulders, my waist. My hand is a pale green movement touching the sand I can't see. I pull my legs under, reverse, rocket in a face full of bubbles to the surface, a mirror and a bowl holding just a pebble of the sky. Treading, I see my mother wave from the beach, her scarf saying *Careful, careful*, her arm a metronome. I raise my arm to wave and then feel it, the current slam flat into my chest. For a moment, I'm under, in the rush, and then popping up again. My mother walks into the water watching. Her legs scissor and disappear in the froth. I put my face in the water then, pull with my arms, kick my legs, keeping the shore to my left as I'd been taught to. The water pushes under my belly, against my side. My mother is smaller, the details of her face disappearing. I turn my head to breathe, kick and go left, breathe and kick. The sun makes a fist on the back of my head, my hair tentacles out of its braid and into my eyes. I am safe at last when I feel the way the water washes not out to sea but back and forth against itself again. Diving, still moving left but now left and shoreward, I exhale, kick hard towards the lighter, greener water still to my left, straightening out. When my feet touch the sand with my eyes above the waterline, I lie in the white foam, letting it wash me back to my mother.

***

We are bailing rainwater with plastic pails when the Coast Guard ship, three times our size, materializes out of the sluice of an afternoon sky. The rain fills our boat. It bobs and tips in six-foot seas less and less buoyantly. An hour or so before, we watched the storm-front drop a veil of gray cotton into the waves. My father twisted the key in the ignition, the motor spun over and died. He stumped down the aft steps and hung over the side; my brother, still getting out of his goggles, put them on again and flipped back over the gunwale. The bow pointed to the horizon clotting up and going green. I shivered from the deck, wrung out my hair, braided it again. "Waterspouts," I say, pointing as bits of cloud drop into the water, spin, dissolve, reform. My older brother comes up with the prop and a handful of hardware. My father shrugs on a tank again, drops backward. The wind picks up, the men surface, plink bits of metal in a box by the prop, submerge. I follow them down the anchor line, meet them just below the drive shaft. They winnow the sand with their hands, pick up everything bright. I bring it to the surface, once, twice, again. Each time I surface, the sky is lower, the boat less on its keel, more tipped on its edges. At last the men rise too, drape themselves in towels, my father putting the little pieces together. Lightning strikes on the horizon. My father shakes his head, "We don't have all of it." My brother grabs the radio handset. The lightning comes again in two places, just west of us and right in front. It leaps up from the water, fingered like tree roots, blinding, deafening. Our boat lurches, bends, groans, the dive gear clanging against itself in its rack. *Mayday*, my father says calmly into the handset, *M'aidez.*

***

We dive a young reef, a wreck just going fan-coral and animals. In the boat, my father fixes the fog in his mask with spit, then tosses his speargun into the water; it rides a minute before sinking. We drop down the anchor rope, following it to the sea floor. He grabs the gun by its barrel, his hand a white anemone almost glowing. The sun above me at twenty feet is a silver circle of barracuda. Their teeth are arrays of knives, their eyes shift and click, shift and click. My air tastes metallic and sweet. At forty feet the refracted light buckles and bends, little round mirrors of exhaled air rise and join and unfold at the surface. My father hunts; I play, corkscrew and flip through the water, touch the barnacles and corals, let tiny fish run between my fingers. Ten minutes in, my father hands me his stringer of dying fish writhing around the rope through their gills. I hang the thing on a chunk of wrecked metal as my father disappears. I am looking at the surface through a cloud of my own air when he rockets around the hull, his eyes rounds of black. He is saying something but of course I don't understand until I see behind him the barracuda he has shot, its guts threaded around the spear in its side, its eyes lit with dying. It gasps the water in, open and close, pumping it over gills that leak inky brown blood. My father whooshes by me, but the barracuda stays on course, a dart pointed at my heart. It's ten feet from me, nine, and I'm thinking, *This fish is going to kill me*, it's eight feet long at least, rough-toothed and sharp, and five feet from me, and four feet. I start screaming, the scream a curtain of bubbles, but the fish keeps coming. I scream and scream. The barracuda is two feet from me, and one. It's a dream the sudden way it plunges downward dead on the sand at my feet, one eye on the seabed, the other watching its kin at the surface, circumnavigating the sun.

***

The thermometer registers 104°, my back is a waterfall of shivers, my arms won't sit still. Chuck takes my temperature. Takes it again. He lays a hand on my forehead, thinking it's something more than measuring. "It's just a fever," I say, teeth clenched. He puts another blanket on top of the comforters on top of the blanket on top of another blanket, a flannel nightgown, then pajamas. "It's just a fever." I turn to look at the lamplight, which humps across the tabletop. *Worms,* I say, *there are worms, there are worms.* But I have not said this out loud, and in any case, he is gone, miles away, through the archway into the bathroom to fill the tub. I can see that his back bent over the edge is a horse's leg. He paws the ground, nostrils steaming. I say, "the toast is burning." I say, "what is on fire here?" I say, "I'm so cold." The horse lifts its foreleg, rushes towards me, I see how the leg has eyes, one greenish brown, the other golden, these are Chuck's eyes. I say out loud, "I'm so cold, Chuck, help me." His hand is ice on my forehead, his arm is under my knees and the other under my shoulders, there is a rush of air, "never mind the clothes," he says, "never mind," he says. He lays me in the bathtub as if into a sun-warmed field of violets and clover, the water is warmer than my skin, it is sea-salty, the tub so large I can lie flat. I feel his fingers unbuttoning my clothes, I feel the way he eases my elbow out of my wet dress, I feel the way the dew in this field becomes the sea, and how my hair, loosed from its elastic, catches his fingers in the current. My tears are just the sea burning through me. "Chuck," I say, "Chuck, what are the mermaids saying?" But he has gone and in his place, my mother, her hair alive in a wind of water, her tail a question mark flopping on the tile, her mouth singing, *Shhh, baby, shhh.*

***

I am a child, sitting on the floor beside the couch on which my mother has gone to sleep. I have three books open, all of them about pirates. I am writing in them with a black crayon, owning them with my name, which I cannot yet write. I am trying for any letter I know, this time the letter M, having failed at Es. I scrawl humps in the sea under these boats full of bright-colored and harmless men whose skull-and-crossbones is a cartoon. Above me, my mother's breathing quickens, she jolts her hand, the one with its rings, her leg runs, a dreaming dog's leg. I know better than to wake her, so I lean over and lay my fat palm on her cheek, I say quietly what she has said to my brother, his terrors nearly nightly: "It's just a dream, just a dream, it's okay." Her eyes open, all pupil for a moment. She sits bolt up. She says to no one: "We have to get out of here, the river's rising, we have to get out of here." I drop the crayon. She takes my hand and for a moment her dream materializes, the killing floods of her childhood lapping the threshold. My sudden baby tears are stars plopped on my t-shirt. She breathes, she wakes herself. "It was a dream," she says, dropping my hand, "just a dream." She rises, slowly, from the sofa, I follow her to the kitchen. She sets out milk and shortbread and then calls her own mother, whose soft voice murmurs through the wire. My mother's face relaxes, she is so close to crying just in fear. The sun bakes the orange trees in the backyard a dark green. The cookies she sets out for me feel like sand between my teeth.

***

I leave her, her eyes wide and blank as they always are now in her lost-girl ending, in the hotel bathroom, the shower warming itself, her warming in the steam. "Don't touch me," she says, "I can do it, don't you dare touch me." Her trembling lower lip is an empty sign, I can't tell how she feels, what she knows, whether she *can* do it. But she has strapped herself to independence, so I lay her diaper on the sink, I lay her fresh clothes nearby, bra on top, in the order she'll put them on. "I'll come get you in half an hour," I say. "Just shout if you need me, I'm right above you." I close the bathroom door, my last view is her with her walker, her hands on the buttons of her pajama top. In my room, I sit on the edge of the bed, drop my shoes off, stare into nothing. Behind me, the window is lit with afternoon sunshine, the curtains sepia blocks of light. I lie back, watch the light on the ceiling, an amber moving with the leaves in the wind. The light has left when I startle awake, I have been gone too long. Downstairs, my heart a blur of fear, I open the door to the debacle, her writhing on the flooded floor, dizzy and mouth gaping, blood from the cut on her head on the wall, on the toilet, on her arms bluing with fresh bruises, her left arm tangled in the sleeve she could not get free of, her pajama bottoms a sodden mess wallowing under her knee. Her naked body is white and cold, hairless and wet as a slippery fish. I hand her towel after towel to sop with. I say, "Mom, Mom, I'm so sorry, I'm so sorry. Why didn't you shout, why didn't you say?" Quiet, deliberate, self-contained, she begins to dry herself as if I am not there, humming a song I don't know. The lake around her hips ripples with her motion, her blood blooming on the white towel.

***

When the rain empties itself out of a lowered sky in Rhode Island, refilling the river, the bay, the sea with its uncanny whales sliding along the hook of the Cape, I am transported back to Florida, to the house by the bay that Chuck and I, newly married, loved. Back I go to the hurricane seasons in the early 2000s, each weekend nailing up plywood and hefting sandbags, each week, stowing them again, those summers and autumns working in tandem, oxen pulling the plow, wheels on either end of an axle, two arms, two eyes, as one body. Where I am alone now, years later, the rain sluices, pings, pounds, rattles in the downspouts, damps the basement. My head is a bog full of ghost lights bound to drown me, I walk toward them, arms open. There were times in Florida when the stars sat just on the roof joists, close as sparklers in your hand. We lay warm nights together on the roof sometimes, shoulders touching, heads bent together, silent as that sky, watching it wheel. He could name the stars, he could draw with a finger the lines that bound them, ley lines, ghosting over the dark. When he died, I believed him among them, particularly in Orion, the hunter and his dog, particularly (I told myself) in the light of Orion's right shoulder. Chuck was an archer, too, his face in my mind a still cameo bisected by the bowstring, his dart paraboling to the target, piercing a spot small and orange as Betelgeuse. The feather on the arrow is a bird thrown suddenly into flight; his elbow, raised and tense, is a wing.

***

I am five hundred miles north of him when he stops breathing, blood from a cut on his hand smeared on the bathroom walls, the tub, the floor, the doorway. I close my eyes to sleep a few feet from the abattoir evidence of his dying. In the hard dark behind my eyelids, he shows me not what happened, but his body in a running river, the surface glassy and lucid, his face bubbled over with air he could not breathe, is not breathing. He does not see me seeing him. The water over him rushes and whirls somewhere else but is perfectly still where he lies, his eyes wide with shock and unblinking, the whites perfectly clear around his moss-colored irises, behind his glasses; his mouth is a round of surprise, in the muscles between his eyebrows, perplexity. Just days before, I'd reached out a finger to rub the spot, "Hey," I said, hey. "What's this? Cut that out." He'd laughed and chased me through the house until we crashed, giggling on the sofa, the dogs zooming past us. His face underwater is still. I say, "Wake up, wake up." I try to touch him, but I have no hands. I hear in my head: *This is what it feels like here.* I say: *Is it cold? Can you breathe?* He says: *Oh sweetheart, I drowned, I drowned dry in the air.* His voice weeps. He once told me how, when he was a child on the Severn River, he swam without breathing, the full width of it. On the other side, there were limestone banks full of fossils, the imprint of animals with swirling shells or fans or scallops. With his finger he traced them over and over, in wonder. He took a chunk of this rock and carried it home. It sits in my lap now, soft and powdering my black dress, his cat beside me sleeping, this dog he never knew, all of us just up the way from the water to the sea. I hold my breath as long as I can, I hold him in my mind as long as I can. My hand lies still among clusters of lamp-shells and crinoids mineralized to stone.

Rats

It's difficult, impossible really, to live on acreage in a rural place and draw a firm line. This side: orderly, civilized, tidy, and clean. That side: wilderness. Some days, you mow the patch of lawn in front of the woods, admire its smoothness, its edge of sweet clover left for the bees. Other days, the sick possum under the trees hisses and staggers or the hawk snatches a sparrow and eats it at your picture window, feathers like a flurry of petals and the sparrow not dead yet. Fattened with rats, the king snakes grow longer than the broomstick you use to push them back into the tangles of privet and muscadine vines. You've seen these rats, their babies anyway, in a nest in the back of the yard under the trees, a nest dug out in the warm center of a pile of leaves. How like larvae they are, wet and pink and naked, so that you cover them up again in hopes that the world is tenderer than you know it is. You can't kill anything that vulnerable, that like an unboned thumb. Later, when you check on the nest, they're gone; the hollow where they lay lined in the fur you'd combed from your dogs earlier in the Spring.

One summer day, a hump in the flower box caught my eye, the fiber liner in disarray, the dirt and moss-rose bellied up. I'd planted the moss-rose in the Spring, and in the heat it had just begun to put out its throat-pink blooms. I could not imagine what had lifted the plants that way, almost free of the dirt, the roots exposed, pale silk threads thicker than spiderwebs, but only just. The pearlized bits in the potting soil looked like pellets of bone. The dirt spilled out of the flowerbox into a cone-shaped pile on the ground underneath as if it had been running through an hourglass, keeping time. I don't know what I thought that hump in the flower box was besides wrong, bad for the flowers. *I'll get the hose*, I thought, *water them in good and it'll be fine.* But as I stepped forward, the flowers shifted slightly, then the whole box rattled hard. I couldn't register fast enough why this should be before the box came alive with rats, rats boiling over the edge of it, rats running across my shoes past me out the open screen door into the yard, through the lattice holes in the pen wall, leaping the stone wall into the flowerbeds, climbing up the lattice, dashing behind the coop. It was as if the world had suddenly revealed itself to be composed solely of rats who only needed a push to reveal themselves.

I thought: *Scream!* I just stood there, silent, rooted in surprise, the rats running everywhere squeaking their horror-show squeaks.

***

When this happens, I am clutching a pail of dirt full of worms to spread in the pen for the chickens, my hand balled into a fist around the handle. Minutes later, I stand in the house in my dirty shoes with this pail and a look on my face.

"Chuck," I say. I am still very calm. "We have rats."

"I know, I know. You mean out back?"

"No, I mean: *We have rats.* In the coop. Everywhere."

"Everywhere? In the house you mean?"

"I don't know, I don't know. They're *everywhere.*" My head feels light like an empty plastic bag, like the tide is out but it is coming in fast. "They just poured out of the flower box on the coop. Poured. Out of the flower box. On me. *On me.*"

"Show me. It'll be okay."

We walk to the coop at the corner of the house, I am imagining rats everywhere, in everything, rat faces in the grass, rat tails in the trees, rat droppings on the pavement, everything blinks and skitters. I set the pail of dirt down in the chicken pen while Chuck looks at the flower box, its contents now fully upended on the ground, the liner like it had been roiled in an accident. The uprooted moss-roses are starting to wilt, I see how the stems look just like the slender, hairless tails of rats.

"Look here," Chuck says. He's crouched where the coop meets the house. Beside the coop, pieces of hay from the chickens' nests fringe a hole in the dirt.

"Oh god. They're under there now?"

"Can't be. Wire's okay"—he pulls some near the hole to make sure it isn't loose or broken. "Small ones maybe, though, until they're too big to get back in."

To keep out vermin, like rats, he'd built the coop over a foundation wrapped in wire dug a foot down in the dirt. But the wire-holes are big enough for lizards, snakes—small rats.

"Look," I say, pointing at a tiny pink nose, a spray of gray whiskers poking out of the wire. I have to remind myself: rats are bad, bubonic plague, hanta fever, *disease disease disease.* I call up images of plague buboes the size of oranges and black as burnt flesh, babies eaten in their cribs, people with leprosy waking up a little less themselves for rats gnawing off numb fingers in the night. What rats can do to chickens, eat them alive, piece by piece. The baby-rat under the coop sniffs at us, his bead-dark eyes unblinking.

"He's so small," Chuck says. "A baby."

The baby has basilisked me motionless. It takes the sudden sound of my dogs barking in the house to bring me back.

***

A few hours later we stand in our local feed-and-seed, looking at all the ways one can move rats on, say, to the rat-afterlife, if there is one. Or, say, to the wilderness beyond the creek a couple of football fields or more behind our house. We decide against every device that seems cruel, against insides-melting poisons, against horrifying glue-traps that force the rat's head down and slowly suffocate it. We're not those people, the anything-but-rats people. We're the people trying to negotiate a healthy relationship with the wild, trying to find that line between our space, safety, order, cleanliness, and health, and the space in which rats figure. We want to be civilized about it, to be civil to the rats, but to move them *on.*

We buy a nine-inch catch-cage, a wire rectangle with a bait latch that, tripped, locks the rat in the cage for transport elsewhere. The first night we set it out, we catch an adult right outside the coop, six or so inches long, tail like a thick, pale taproot. Chuck drives it miles from home and releases it into a field. We set the trap out again the next night and many nights afterward, but we never catch another one. We decide that this means they've crossed over, gone back to the woods in the way-back, to the leaf piles, the predictable hazards of snakes and hawks and feral cats.

So when a little while later Chuck opens the door to the walk-in space under the house and hears rustling coming from under the plastic grill-cover on the grill-pad nearby, he expects lizards, a trapped bird, something benign.

Now, this is the part of the film where you know what you shouldn't do, the part where, as the audience, you know what comes next but the characters never seem to. You know the serial killer is in the darkened

72

basement. That the sound you're hearing is the demon-possessed doll spooling up. That the house is going to collapse. That the ticking noise is a timer on a bomb. You know you should run, that the worst decision you can make is not to run, fast, far, whatever else—away.

But when the rustling starts under the plastic, Chuck is not you. He's Dead Teenager Seven, Zombie Bait Five, Unsuspecting Space Soldier Twelve. He does not run away. Instead, he ambles over and puts his hand on the grill and triggers an explosion.

Inside the house, I hear bald, naked, panicked screaming. In the seconds it takes me to get to the door, I imagine severed arteries spurting great gushes of blood, a bashed-in blood-spattered head, fingers caught in a saw, ripped ragged but still twitching. It's that kind of screaming. I run to the door. The dogs are there first, barking and whining and scratching. I push them with my legs, Chuck is bleeding out right then, and I can't get the door open and then I do and we're launched into the sunlight on the deck. The dogs are like missiles, straight-arrowing low to the ground, tails flat out like lances, hurtling towards the grass. Chuck stands, unbloodied, not screaming anymore but pacing, muttering, brushing at his pants, his arms, his hair. The dogs zigzag in the grass, Blue, the furry red Akita mix, doing figure-eights; the gray Catahoula leopard dog, Ollie, making endless parentheses cupped in parentheses. They're boiling up the grass, but I see only that Chuck is not dead, that he has all his fingers, that there is no blood.

"What happened? What happened? Are you okay?"

"Rats," Chuck says. "So many rats. In the grill. God, the rats. No, no bites. I'm okay. Really I'm—"

By the end of that sentence, we're both watching the dogs, we've turned towards the yard where they're making figures in a small, moving patch of grass and sun, the red dog with his head down, lifting and coming down hard now on his front legs, the gray-spotted dog concentrated on the edges, packing in the edges, keeping the center tight against the red dog's legs. Inside the edges he's making, the grass is teeming, boiling, bubbling with gray bodies that pop into the air like the ground is on fire.

At that moment, Blue understands his job, understands it with a kind of passion reserved for vocation, for the perfect moment when the purpose of being becomes clear. Ollie always knew, was always doing his job: Blue discovers his. He puts his head into the squirming grass, the rats popping onto his face now, his ears flattened, his lips drawn back. He snatches a rat delicately, as though testing a bit of lace with his front teeth, the rat nearly as big as his snout, the other rats racing under him, him bouncing straight-legged to keep them down, and the rat is in his mouth, struggling. Even from this far, you can see it lash its tail, its paws scrabbling at the dog's jaw.

In a second Blue goes absolutely still, the rat in his mouth squealing, trying to get free. The dog tenses up, then looses the kinetic energy in his neck in one short snap. The rat hangs limp. The dead body tossed aside, Blue reaches down again, Ollie keeping the pack tight against his legs, he picks up another, whip-breaks its neck, tosses it, and another, and another. When the pack begins to loosen, four or five rats left maybe, Ollie begins cutting single rats from the herd and pushing them towards Blue. The survivors streak for the trees, Ollie fast behind them, cutting left, cutting right, no time for his sheep-stare but plenty for his best side-to-sides that turn the rat back to its end. Blue keeps right where Ollie can see him, takes up each rat, kills it so quickly you nearly miss that sideways snap of his head, the graceful arcing of the dead body into a tidy, motionless pile a few feet from his work.

In less than a minute, the rats are gone, one or two back in the woods where they belong, the rest quiet, lying on their sides like this was sleep. We get the dogs into the house, pet them elaborately, praise them, inspect Blue's face for bites or scratches. I call the vet to see if he needs to be vaccinated. "No," she says, "but congratulations. You could rent him to some folks we know." I laugh. I can see him with the rats, I remember his puppyhood, his sweet handsome face with its emphatic eyeliner. I'm not sure how to reconcile that with the death-machine he's clearly meant to be. Once the dogs are settled in, Chuck and I go inspect the corpses in the yard. "Dozen," he says. "More," I say. "What do we do with them?"

"Other things can eat them, right?"

I was not thinking of them as food. I say nothing. Chuck walks outside the gate to a small hillock where a pine tree stump sticks up from the moss like a table. The tree had been eaten through with pine beetles, all one hundred feet of it, so we'd had it removed when we moved in several years before. "Here," he says. "We can set them out here." He gets waterproof garden gloves and lifts the rats by their tails, still flexible and cooling, into the wheelbarrow, then sets them in a pattern on the stump, like a flower, their tails all curled toward the center, their perfect bodies like petals. None looks a bit disheveled. "Are they even dead?" I say. "They don't look dead." Chuck lifts one and shakes it a little. It's clearly not living.

There are more than twenty of them, so he layers them. "Zinnia," I say. There is no blood anywhere, no color—the rats are shades of gray and brown, their button eyes dimmed and open, even their noses without pink. They make a zinnia of meat in black and white on the old stump. Above us, our family of crows gathers. They are almost perfectly quiet except for the sound of their wings, five of them, the parents and two generations of grown children. We had watched them hatch and fledge; they knew us and alerted us to threats to the chickens in the yard or called out when we were gardening and they were ready to descend on the grubs we'd dug up.

I wave at them, one startling briefly in a half-caw. "Hi," I say. "Hi, crow-babies. Dinner's served." Chuck laughs, lifts the last corpse by its tail. It's a young male, each foot perfect, each toe perfectly defined, the nails flecks of white. Chuck curves him into the shape the dogs make sleeping, their noses tucked under their tails, sets him in the middle of the flower like a heart. "Sleep well," he says, giving it a pat. In the morning, when we check, none of the bodies remains.

Sexing Chicks

"I don't know," I say. "I think this one's legs are more tooth-pick-y."

At that point, I had never held an actual baby chicken, but now I have one in each hand, and it's so hard to keep them there, they squirm and protest. It's like trying to hang onto tiny, frightened toddlers without squeezing them to death or dropping them. In a big blue Rubbermaid bin lined with pine shavings and paper towels, about sixty week-old birds press themselves flat under red-hot heating lamps or dash-wobble in circles. They peep like the insane, in a pitch that would call dogs, at decibels like a dozen car alarms taped straight to the head. My two have open, beige-y beaks with little pink tongues, orange-colored legs below fluffy, butter-colored butts. I squint at their legs each time they stop kicking.

The chicken vendor—Laura—and I are leg-sexing to locate the future hens. I can't have roosters, they're too noisy, too potentially violent, too hard to keep happy, and they're not necessary since all I want is pest control and some eggs. Laura says that boys can have thicker shanks, so we're looking for the thinnest—the girliest—chick-legs in this particular hatch.

"I don't know. What about this one?" Laura holds a puff of down in her hand, pulls its leg gently so the shin is extended across her palm. I move my two chicks next to hers. We both bend closer, trying to compare.

"If it's skinnier, it's not much skinnier," I decide. She nods her head, puts her chick back in the bin where it squeaks, then runs, ricocheting off the sides until it crashes into a group of other birds. It finally settles under the heat lamp, its wing-nubs spread flat. Laura grabs another one.

"How about this one?" The leg is yellow and minutely scaled. The chick peeps and struggles.

We decide it's a girl who joins two others in the big cardboard box I'm taking home. I'll set them for a few weeks under a heat-lamp in a blue bin just like the one they came from, then move them to the coop outside. I've become a hen keeper.

It's an entirely new identity. I don't come from farmers. In fact, I never knew any farmers growing up, never went to a farm, never had plastic farm animals and a plastic barn though I did have a See-and-Say that mooed and crowed. But this is exotic, like food from other places. My immediate family is white-collar suburban. Except for corn on the cob, our vegetables came from cans or the freezer. Our meat came cut up and wrapped in plastic. Before I reached adulthood, I had never seen livestock up close except in petting zoos and then of course I made no connection between the huge hot animal I was stuffing carrots into and the London broil Mom grilled later that night.

Sexing our few pets was easy or immaterial. The gerbils came solo, no sex in the cages, so no need to know whether "Gerbil" was a girl or a boy. With the dogs and cats, we depended on the names our parents gave them, or kittens suddenly appeared, so we knew. It's only after I get my chickens that my mother tells me about a strange aunt who might have had a flock in the 1940s up in the hills near the town where my parents grew up. It's the first I've heard of it. "Aunt Jen had chickens?" I say. "Oh yes," my mother responds, "I think I remember chickens. Yes, and I collected eggs, maybe. Anyway, there were chickens, I imagine. She had everything else."

In the '40s in the Alleghenies, sexing chickens wouldn't have mattered much. When they were big enough to tell cockerel from pullet, my great-aunt would have counted up what she had (the ideal ratio is a single rooster for about eight hens) and eaten the extra males. In that context, it can't matter that until they're about four months old, only experts— specifically people who stare at millions of tiny chicken butts all day looking for a miniscule vent-pimple that's the future rooster's "penis"— can guess if your chicks will lay.

I started doubting leg-sexing that first day, crouching on the floor doing my best to guess. I had little information, no training, and no faith in the method we used. Laura, who said it would work, was the faithful. Me, I left with only anxiety and three chicks in a brown cardboard box.

Virtually every day after I brought them home, I'd pick them up, look them over, and decide pessimistically: "They're all male. I know they're all male." Then I'd thumb through my chicken books or get my computer and start cruising chick-sexing videos trying to learn how I might know for sure.

Amateur chicken sexing depends on gender stereotyping, the belief that hens are docile, fearful, and quiet, that roosters fight back. To ring-sex or penny-sex, you dangle rings on threads above the chickens' heads (the still rings indicate hens) or drop a penny and see who scatters (the hens run away). I'd played the ring game over many a pregnant human belly and knew that besides its irrationality, subsequent births revealed a high prediction-failure rate. Though I could imagine how a bunch of hens might be afraid if I dropped, say, a hatchet in their midst, I couldn't imagine how a penny would frighten anyone. In surfing de-hoaxing-chicken-sexing posts, I very quickly found the picture I knew existed: dozens of certified hens not crouched in terror or fleeing to the hills, but bent over inspecting the coppery profile of Abraham Lincoln. Old Honest Abe wasn't going to help me here.

Maybe six or seven weeks in, about the time I start dreaming of the chickens trying on my clothes and coming home from school with ZZ Top beards, I attempt a few tests. I need to know. I'm not going to kill the boys, but I need to know.

"What are you doing with her?" Chuck says. He's got his mug of coffee and the paper, has come out to visit the coop.

I'm holding the pre-pubescent Jadzia in the crook of my arm the way I always do. Just over her eyes she has a tiny, orangey-pink comb, though the two little scoops of wattle coming in on her chin are still beige-yellow, the color of her legs. She bobs her head and chuckles, pecks at my ring. I am afraid the darkening of her comb means she's a boy, though the smallness of her wattles gives me hope. I ruffle her neck-feathers, just going coppery.

"What am I doing? I'm dipping the chickens."

"What? Why?"

"Holding them upside down by their legs for a second. People say if you do this, the hens will stay calm; the roosters will flap around trying to get loose. Because I need to know if I've got roosters. Because I need to find homes for them if I have roosters. Because I need to know."

Chuck looks at me, sips his coffee. I take this as permission to proceed.

I reach up under Jadzia and hold her legs. Then, carefully, I let her body drop into an exaggerated dip. She flaps like crazy. I begin to cry.

"It's a rooster. I know it. She's a rooster."

I put her down where she fluffs herself to shake it off. Then she trots over to the others kicking and foraging in the leaves. One of them catches an enormous spider, whose legs jerk and twitch before it's swallowed. I wipe my face. "At least they're taking care of the ticks," I say, "boys or no boys."

Sexing chicks before the eggs come is divination, magic, voodoo, Gestalt guesswork. Leg-sexing and wing-sexing—looking for incipient feather-doubling on the wings of very young chicks—is guessing from the body. So is sizing up combs and wattles and watching for spurs. The naked face-flesh of males is big and red, except when it isn't (in some individuals and in some breeds). Before their first year, most roos grow a fourth or fifth toe with a nail like a razor half-way up their shanks. But some hens can grow them and some roos never do. Then there's feathering. Many hens have rounded feathers on their backs and necks, some have pointed ones, some have frizzed or hairy ones. Some roos have long fountains of tails in green, orange, salmon, and black. Some don't. Then there's crowing. Some of the boys crow. Some chicks crow. Many hens crow. Crowing by itself is a crap-shoot, too.

Before point-of-lay at about twenty weeks, or sometimes twenty-eight, or sometimes sixteen, the best way to sex a chicken is to examine its genitals. About ninety percent of the time, expert sexers get it right. They turn the young bird upwards and invert its cloaca (the excretory and reproductive pouch for birds), see if it's got the tiny bump that's the bird's sperm-delivery system. Amateurs get it wrong, mostly. But I try anyway.

At about three months in, no closer to an answer, I hold Rebeaka, the placid one who comes anytime I call and likes to sit next to me on the rocker. "Look," I tell her, "I'm never going to eat you. But I really do like you. And I want to know if I can keep you." I feed her a handful of grapes. She takes them stoically, one at a time, pumping her head to get them down her throat. I know she understands. "I have to know if you're a boy. Because crowing isn't allowed. Because this is a nice neighborhood and I can't have crowing." I'm not sure who I'm talking to, really.

I have been studying pictures of chicken vents for weeks, obsessively. Drawing them so I can memorize the subtle differences. At last I think I know what a boy-chicken looks like from behind, all those pictures with the little hump on the lower lip, the little pearl of semen. These grapes and this chat are my way of trying to convince Rebeaka to let me take a look at her ass, which will require her compliance for a few seconds. She gulps down another grape, turns one deep-amber eye, then the other, waiting to see if I have more food to give her. When I pick her up, she tucks her neck into her body and half-closes her eyes.

Very carefully, still holding her body, I tip her over, her head downwards, her feet toward my stomach. Her tail feathers spread and she squawks a little, her legs pumping. She tries to free her wings and right herself. For a second, I think I see something, but then she's squirming so much I can't tell for sure. I can't convince myself that's what I've seen. She's struggling and squawking now, one wing free and flogging my forearm. I set her on the ground and find her some mealworms, a kind of payment for the indignity. She follows me around the yard like a dog, tut-tutting and pecking at the grass.

Chuck calls from the deck, "Girl or boy?" I say, "I'm pretty sure she's a girl." I'm not, of course.

In fact, I'm not sure until several weeks later. It's morning, early. I'm out cleaning the coop, taking the spent hay and droppings to the compost heap. I have the bucket when I hear a strange choking from across the yard. Think Andre the Giant trying to catch your attention across a football field, think Luciano Pavarotti with bad congestion projecting his sinus-clearing to the back of the balcony. I think: "What the hell animal is that?" We have two acres of trees, minks, foxes, raccoons, all kinds of things in the jungly backyard beyond our creek. I think: one of the dogs is vomiting. I start running under the trees toward the back door when it happens again. Only it's different this time. More music in the cough. More—crow. When Henrietta does it a third time, I'm standing there watching her. She lifts on her toes, flaps her wings a couple of times, stretches her neck, and opens her beak like a megaphone.

What comes out is a hoarse, croaky imitation of a cartoon rooster-crow. The effect on Henrietta is electric. She has no idea what's going on, what's possessed her, why this noise is coming out of her. Each time she crows, and she does it with greater and greater proficiency, she looks startled, out of control of her body, like you could knock her over with a feather. She runs in tight circles, blinking frantically, flapping her wings spastically so they hit her in the face. Once she bowls straight into Rebeaka, who, after a brief consideration, opens her beak and croaks out a weak imitative bark, then a full-throated roar-crow. She's so startled by this she topples over sideways, kicks her feet, and squawks. She hops up, runs toward me, then back under the deck, then back to me, tucks herself next to my leg and shivers.

I think: this must be just like when boys get their first erections. That kind of mystical crazy.

The roosters, the two of them, shake themselves finally and begin practicing strutting. Or maybe they've been strutting for a while, I don't know. Suddenly the fragments come together. I notice they have testicular, dangling wattles and bright red combs, Henrietta's hanging rakishly over an eye. Their tails have started to arch and droop, and they both have thick rows of fur-like feathers over their shoulders and backs. Neither's laid an egg. Boys. I have two boys.

Jadzia, the sole hen, is the only one of us not startled by the crowing, knowing all about it, as she probably has all along.

In the Wake

I could picture exactly where Edie was when she called. I'd stood on that very spot in the upstairs hall of her house in Madison, about an hour from mine when we both worked in Wisconsin. She was lying just between the bathroom and back bedroom where there was a quilt on the wall and the eaves pitched inwards and the window spilled yellow light onto the wood floor.

"I just wanted to let you know," she said.

"What?" I was brushing my teeth, so this came out, *Wha?*

"It's about the turkey baster."

"Turkey baster?" *Tuhkey bastew?* I spat. I repeated.

She giggled. "I'm here," she said, "with the turkey baster. We just did it."

I knew what she was talking about, she'd been talking about it for weeks, making sure the sperm got to her cervix, making sure there were enough to make a baby. Squirting it in there, high and deep. It required concentration. The leaflet she showed me stressed postcoital calm.

Instead she was yukking it up with me. I had a vision of her half-dressed and giddy in her hall, her naked backside on a bolster. In one hand, Edie held the used turkey baster with its testicular bulb and clear plastic shaft. In the other, her phone. It was just too ridiculous. I had to sit down.

"Oh my God. Edie, stop it. I can't breathe."

"No seriously, I've got my legs up in the air now—"

"Edie, sweet Jesus, stop. If you laugh like this, you know you'll just squirt it out and have to do it over again—"

"Oh shit," she said, her voice muffled by movement, "too late—"

We were howling so hard that the phone went to static on both ends.

That summer, we drove to the local state park for a picnic. We climbed a big pile of rocks, nearly a mountain, up makeshift stairs cut into the side. The dog's toenails scrabbled for purchase on the stones, it was that precarious. We sucked air, grabbed saplings with our bare hands to hoist ourselves up the next bit, and the next. Another friend, gripped by acrophobia, shakily descended from part way up clutching each stair down, her long scarf hanging up on the scrub beside the path. Edie and I and the dog climbed all the way to the top. She said to me: "This is why I come up here, for the perspective," her hands on her hips.

From the path that ran across the ridge some ten or twenty feet off the absolute edge, I could see the black circle of the lake, the flat round pupil of an eye looking up at us, the tree tops small and brushy, and the filmy clouds overhead hung in pure blue sky. Edie walked straight to the very edge, studded with boulders. She leaned way over to look for our friend, invisible in her green clothes against the green canopy above the green scribbles of grass. Edie said: "Should we send the dog down so she has company?" I said: "He won't go, he loves you too much."

And here's what I really remember about this day, about this moment: how Edie came back from the edge of that abyss in two long bounds, joyful at being preferred above everyone, in her dog's pure love. How she knelt in the dust, her bare knees with their rubbing of freckles, how she knelt and called her dog to her, how she beat her palms together, kissing the air, and when he came to her, how she grabbed him by the shoulders and ruffled his spaniel ears and kissed that dog's face like she had never thought once of leaving him. I remember the thick brush of his tail in the light, the back and forth of it winnowing the air, and I wish I had thought of this, this tail, this dog, this moment with her in between the dust and the golden air, when I spoke to her last.

I didn't know how thirsty she was, but I should have known because I'd seen the way she set about doing everything else, running flat out with both hands full, the long muscles of her pushing against the earth so that she might fly. When we lived near the beach, I discovered that she drank this way, too.

Chuck and I took her to where the Gulf of Mexico lapped the coast, west of Tampa. She needed a suit, so before we did anything else, we found a shop for tourists, half-buried in the sand like a treasure chest. Stepping into the air-conditioned store from the heat outside was like entering the Antarctic. We stood and shivered a moment, orienting ourselves. Merchandise lay in heaps, falling off hangers, a stray strap hanging here, a tumbled pair of shorts there, crumpled as if they'd been kicked off just then. Edie beelined for a boy-legged suit in blue and white. She bought the matching hat and a pair of white, oval sunglasses that hid nearly all her face, and changed her clothes right there. Stepping out of the store, she held her hat on with her right hand just like a movie star. She looked famous in all that dazzling sun, her eyes hidden, her long neat thighs, her bare feet on the burning pavement. The square openings for her legs cut into her flesh and made her real, like the freckles on her chest did, like the way her front teeth had turned slightly out of line coming in. We trundled onto the sand, flipped the blanket out, settled in. She sat with her magazine while Chuck and I swam.

"Did you hear about the shark attacks in New Jersey?" she said as I shook off the water and rolled down onto the blanket. "I've been reading about them."

"Was anyone killed?"

"Three or four or so."

Must be a great white, I thought. *Nothing to worry about, we don't have those here.* But even so, I tensed a little, as if the word itself were dangerous.

"When did this happen?"

"Before the war."

The water turned itself over once or twice on the shells at the tidemark and I thought, *It's high tide.* But also, *What war?* Three light-haired children screamed and took turns dunking each other in the wash before the sandbar. Their mother lay sleeping on her stomach in the sun, her hair dark with suntan oil and her face turned towards us. Their father netted the water down the beach a bit, called to the children now who turned their heads as if one body to listen. The water made their voices too close, right next to my ear. Out past the sandbar, Chuck's head bobbed up, went under again, bobbed up again. I shaded my eyes to see better where he was.

"War?" I said.

"The Great War, you know, World War I. In New England. They hunted that shark for weeks."

Christ, I thought, *that was ages and ages ago.* "Jesus, Edie, I thought you were talking about recently." Frowning, I felt like I'd wasted something that wasn't very important, but still: I'd wasted it. "Is this research?"

"Sort of," she said. She didn't turn her head. "Doesn't matter, really. The ocean's full of sharks. Everywhere. All the time. They take pictures from helicopters of sharks just swimming with people. They look like seals, but they aren't. They're hunting. You should see them." She wore long silver earrings that moved when she did and broke up the light. She sat up and gripped her knees, looking out at the water, at the children who were now on the shore with blue sand pails and little plastic shovels. The oldest stood over the other two, pointing at the ground, pushing her hair back over her ear, pointing again. She wore a reddish friendship bracelet on her left wrist, its strings dripping water as she gestured. The ruffle on her pink suit blew sideways, and even from here we could see she had gooseflesh and a sunburn. Edie got up and took off her hat, dropped it back on the blanket then stretched like a cat. She left her sunglasses on, but raised one hand to shield her eyes, like a salute. "I'm hot," she said to the horizon, "I think I'll walk for a while." I watched her head north right at the water's edge, her feet kicking up splashes like diamonds, her tall shadow hinged to her feet at her right.

She came back about an hour later, just as I thought we ought to begin looking for her. Chuck had one end of the blanket, shaking the sand out, the wind blowing it everywhere, onto everything. I had her shoes, her magazine, her bag, her hat pressed under my arm. She carried a piña colada with two straws and a silly green parasol stuck in it, a drink accessorized for fun. She lifted and lowered her feet as if she were walking in something sticky, the thick sand creaking under her toes. She'd found the store again and bought a sarong and she looked beautiful, her hair a kind of bleach-tipped fur ruffling in the wind. I couldn't see her eyes. She laughed: "Let's have a drink, shall we?"

***

I woke her from a hard sleep the next day, nearly the last one in her stay— rolled her out of bed and into her suit and into the car with the canoe roped to the top. The air hummed in the cords over the windows as we traveled. At Gandy Beach, we swung the car into the mangroves and parked under a cabbage palm. We set the boat on the ground, loaded up the seats, the cooler, the anchor, gaff, paddles, everything. Chuck took the stern, I took the prow, Edie carried Chuck's coffee and thermos, her sunglasses sitting slightly askew on her nose. The cut at the waterline was empty now, but there'd been a party there lately, beer cans floating, a used condom caught on the mangrove knees, and the remains of a fire.

The canoe slid into the water as if it were oiled. The bottom rasped hollowly over mangrove roots, crushed oyster shells, and gray sand, then went silent except for the tick of brown water against the hull. I stepped in at the back, my feet sandy and wet, my ankles and calves and arms cool and salty. I watched as Edie lifted herself into the center of the boat as if she'd floated there. But something went wrong, the side dipped down too far and she rolled, convulsing with laughter, headfirst into the bilge at the bottom, all laughing and legs tangled in the anchor line. I reached into this to help her sit up, her hand cool in mine, her rings biting my palm then releasing. She adjusted her blue folding seat suspended mid-canoe and sat facing front, then pushed her sunglasses up on her head and made that sucking noise through her teeth that meant she was happy, though there was mud on her shoulder and her shorts, and her shin was scraped bloody. When Chuck got in, he stood for a while in front of the aft bench watching for dimples in the distance, nose prints on the surface. We had more than a mile of paddling to get to the power station exhaust outlet, but the manatees could have been anywhere between, and Chuck wanted to spot the first one. *That or a dolphin*, he said, and Edie giggled and clapped her hands as if this were Christmas and dolphins or manatees made no difference. I dipped into the water on the left side to turn us right. Chuck settled in at the rudder-paddle, each J-stroke quietly thumping the side.

The trip through the mangroves took about an hour and a half, maybe more, maybe less. The sun sat in the tops of the trees, the water washed over and into mangrove roots encrusted with oysters and barnacles, rime-thick. We stopped once to watch a gray thing flick by under the boat, a young shark, a large fish, we couldn't tell. The sunlight filtered through the water to the bottom where the grass looked both green and yellow, bathed in some sort of golden liquor. It waved back and forth, leaning in the direction of the tide. The canoe shadowed it, and in the shadows small fry gathered and darted. Edie put her hand in and took it out again, the drops of water beading down her arm as she ran her wet hand through her hair. When she shook her head, the spray dotted my sunglasses, evaporated immediately, left a pocking of salt and minerals like pinpricks. We navigated by a single landmark, the twin chimneys at the plant. They rose ahead of us to our left, flaring slightly at the top, only one puffing steam. We wove through the trees, through whole habitats, pointing out a kingfisher, a horseshoe crab, a spoonbill, a heron, a wood stork. I hung my legs over, dragged my feet in the water, paddled when Chuck didn't, but mostly I looked at the sky and the water and the trees. We rounded a bend, keeping tight to the hummock, watching the birds stand in the mangroves.

We didn't expect to be alone exactly, but we also didn't expect the half-dozen people fanned out in the warm plume of water coming through the gate at the exhaust outlet. The top of the gate rose about six feet over our heads, disappearing under us, down to the bottom of the cut. Through it we could see the whole length of the canal, meant to cool the water some before it entered the bay, to the plant that sat slumped below its stacks at the end. So far below us that we didn't even register the shadow of it, the exhaust pipe released water powerfully enough that we could stay in place at the bay end of the canal only by holding onto the gate. After a few moments, we let go of it, just let the water take us out, away. Chuck stood aft again. I strained my eyes. We reached the edge of the plume, the ground underneath us still in the dark and invisible, but we began to sense it there now, closer to us, the pressure of it against the water under our keel. Which is when we realized what we were seeing, all of them, all around us. "There they are," Chuck said. Edie squealed. I sat speechless, the paddle over my knees.

Because there were so many—fifty, a hundred, maybe more. I had seen a manatee in the wild before, once, one, in a river. It rolled up to the surface, sent its whiskers up into the air, opened its nostrils and huffed, sunk with its tail lazily up-down and was gone. Here, there were noses everywhere, little and big and every other size. They rose and fell like pistons in a machine, so fast I couldn't count them. They made ripples and small whirlpools with their noses. Right off the prow, I saw a dark form rise like an afternoon dream. I could touch the nose as it came up next to the boat, but I didn't. We were quiet, one rose in the back of the boat, another a few feet from the center. They breathed all around for a quarter mile, came up and breathed and sank again. In the other boats, other people sat and pointed and hushed themselves. Edie stood up behind me to see better, grabbed my shoulder to steady herself, her hand light, then heavy, then light again. I whispered to her: "I've never seen so many." She said: "This is such a gift." I felt her shift her weight to one side of the canoe. "I want to touch them, I want to touch one of them," she said. She knelt by the side of the boat, tipping it a little with her weight, her feet kicking away her chair. Behind her the anchor sat in a scum of bilge water. She waited, her arm bent at the elbow, the black plastic molding on the side of the canoe tucked almost into her armpit. She was rapt and waiting.

It was just then, Edie with her hand out over the water waiting for a manatee to rise under her palm like a magic trick, that a man fishing in a yellow kayak glided by us with a fish on his hook. He struggled to reel it in, a huge fish, an enormous fish because he was a big man in a boat and they were cruising at a clip. His wake had wash. His pole rose, the sound of his reel ticked over, the tip fell, rose, the reel ticked, he glided by. We asked him what he'd caught. "One a them things," he said, "prolly. Seems like anyway. Caint get loose yet, caint drag him aboard." They headed towards the gate and the deep water and there he cut the line. The snap carried across the water like the sound of a broken bone. In our canoe, we sat frozen in a tableau, the look on Chuck's face impossible to describe. Like he was watching a grassfire sweep the horizon toward him and him without even a tumbler of water, like he knew beating that man to death wouldn't make anything different. Instead he made a snorting noise, said something under his breath. Edie and I looked at each other, imagining the manatees below us now, not whole and happy bathing in the warmth with their babies, but each with a fringe of filthy hooks in their tails. Horrified we stared down at the water. All around us they rose and fell still, rolling up from under the boat into view. It's then we noticed how the bigger ones had scars, white like maps on their backs, on their faces. Their eyes, when we saw them, were the same color as the water all around us.

***

Chuck and I stood holding hands, watching Edie's plane lift into a sky so full of thunderclouds it looked mildewed. On the way to the garage, he bought coffee, an oatmeal cookie to share, and a bottle of boutique juice for me. He kept my hand while he paid, dropping it only when he dug out the keys or shifted gears. Our car sped home through a corridor of thick green, punctuated by clusters of palms tipping into the sky, rows of oleanders spitting out poison blooms. Tampa rolled up on our left, buildings poking higher than the trees, lightning coming but not here yet, the air waiting for something to happen, for someone to say something. The silver minarets of the university caught one last glint of light before the clouds closed over the sun. Over the bay, the waves ripped up with the rain, we drove through a river falling out of a sky colicky with thunder. The wipers beat the water back from the glass. In front of us, drivers turned on their hazards, yellow and red lights smearing on the windshield.

Earlier, Chuck had brought me the bottle of vodka. We stood in my study with the neighbor's dog sounding an alarm across the fence, stood in front of the French doors looking out at the garden, him holding the jug between us like a glass plumb bob. Out there, the fig tree and the lemon and the lime, a mockingbird on the grape arbor twitching her tail. Already the heat pouring like water out of a bucket, flattening every color. I looked at Chuck, but he was focused on the birdbath, or the way the mockingbird packed Spanish moss in her mouth like a gag.

"What's wrong?" I asked. I noticed how the gardenia was finally dropping its blossoms.

He showed me the bottle as if I hadn't seen it, though I had. We don't drink hard liquor, so for a minute I didn't know where this bottle had come from, and then I remembered: he'd carted it from Illinois to Wisconsin when we'd married, then from Wisconsin to Florida when we'd moved. We'd never opened it. Last I'd seen it, it was tucked behind some cooking sherry way up over the refrigerator with all the things we didn't use. It had dusty shoulders I felt guilty about, but the vodka in it was clear as water, the seal tight and pasted over with blue paper. Chuck showed me the bottle, tipped it towards me like he wanted me to approve the label. It was three-quarters empty.

"What happened to it?"

"Did your mother drink it?" he asked.

I thought for a minute, shook my head: "She likes wine, not vodka, and she'd have said."

A second passed. Another one.

"Edie's been drinking at night," he said. He was going slowly, being gentle.

She'd been with us three nights. I took the bottle from him. It wasn't dusty anymore, the blue paper was gone and it was mostly empty, but it was still heavy and solid, like flesh. The vodka rocked in its new space, settled back into itself at the bottom.

"Is that a lot? It seems like an awful lot." I wanted him to say *not really*.

"It's a lot, yes," he said. He looked at me through his glasses. He took the bottle then, put it in the kitchen, on the refrigerator next to the sherry, precisely where it had been. Edie woke up a few hours later, had her shower, rolled her suitcase to the door. Got into the car, into the airplane, flew away. She called later that night to tell us she was home. For weeks afterward, every time I walked past the fridge, I thought of the bottle up there like an aneurysm thumping away.

***

Edie was on the phone, calling from the Madison airport, saying she was getting on a plane to come, did we mind? Could she come? Oh, and there was a quilt show in Tampa she wanted to see, she'd gotten tickets for her and me, I'd just love it. Could we get to the beach, too? "Of course, of course," I said, "you're always welcome," and rearranged my schedule. I didn't mind, I was glad to see her.

We drove across the bay to the museum housing the quilt exhibit: a flat concrete slab, its windows vertical under their deep eaves like slits outlined in kohl. We walked down to the river first to look at the hot, summer water lapping against the seawalls, oily and brown and brackish. A tribe of mosquitoes lifted and lowered above the river. The light was thick and orange, not the yellow Edie knew but something denser and almost unendurable. We squinted at each other, at the fragments of sun sparking upward from the wavelets, and then headed indoors without speaking. We cooled off sitting on a bench looking at a quilt that hung by its four corners on the nothing-colored wall. Each patch glowed its own color like stained glass. The pattern's called snake in the grass, but I couldn't follow the snake anywhere. No matter what I looked at, my gaze meandered down to the bound edges and slid off. Edie watched the quilt too, her eyes half closed, her eyelids moving as if she were dreaming.

A Black woman in Kente cloth sat down beside us on the bench. She pointed to the quilt. "That's my great-auntie's."

The cowrie shells in her hair clicked as she turned to look at me. She had yellow irises, her dress was brown and green, and she'd wrapped the same material around her hair high above her brow. Her eyebrows arched way up over her lids almost to the edge of the fabric, and there were ridges across her forehead that meant she worried.

"She didn't like this one much," she said, her eyes flicking between Edie and me and the quilt. Edie nodded as if she understood, but never took her eyes off the wall. I looked away, looked again at the quilt on the wall, traced the pattern to the border again, fell off. The Black woman took an audible breath, then pushed herself up, got close enough to the quilt that the docent suddenly materialized nearby.

"It's that," she said to the quilt. She pointed to a patch no more than a nickel's diameter wide. She could have covered it with her thumb. Her finger accused, not three inches off the piece. The docent edged closer, his hand moving towards the walkie-talkie attached to his shoulder, just in case. She saw him, froze for a moment, then dropped her finger, stepped back, said to the docent who was stopped near her now. "You know she didn't like that one at all."

He said, "No touching, please."

She stepped back another three paces, regarded the quilt with her head canted and her lip pushed out. Then, after one more look at the docent who had folded his arms and was watching her, she moved away into another gallery, her back disappearing. I reached to get my purse, but Edie was suddenly collapsed against my other arm and I couldn't move. She leaned hard into my shoulder. She was cool now, damp cool, the freckles on her shoulder made her look salted. Her bangs had dried sticky with sweat and straight up like a boy's.

"I have to tell you something."

"Sure."

"I saw her out there."

"What, that lady?"

"My mother."

"Your mother? Here?"

"No, in Delaware. I saw her on a tractor. After she died."

I froze as if Edie's mother were standing there right then, passing between me and the quilt I couldn't quite look at anymore, following the Black woman into some other gallery.

"She wanted to talk to me," Edie said. She was doing something with her rings, but I couldn't see what it was. They slid around on her fingers. One of her cuticles looked bitten and red.

"What did she say?"

"Nothing," Edie shrugged. "She didn't really say much at all. That's how I knew it was her."

She told it like a story, her fingers rubbing the hem of her shirt, rubbing a salt stain there, the dried sweat of half an hour ago. She said: "I was out walking in the Fall after she died. I was walking in the fields at the beach house and there was this tractor just sitting there with her in the seat waiting for me to come." Her mother had died in the beach house with

Edie there in the upstairs room. "The sound of her breathing," she said to me as if I would know what she was talking about. "The sound of her breathing was everywhere and then she was dead." In Edie's office in Madison was a picture of her dead mother, young and newly married. She looked all of twenty, a woman from the Northeast of a certain class, a little horsey-faced like her daughter; she wore gloves and a hat, something pale and tailored and perfect for the occasion, whatever it was. The light in the picture was perfect too, shady without darkness.

I imagined it couldn't be exactly under the trees, this green tractor, more sitting in the last light of a short day. I watched in my mind the ghost of Edie's mother sitting on it, waiting to talk to her daughter. She'd hiked herself up onto the seat as if it were comfortable, as if it weren't cold and hard and too high up not to cut into the back of her thighs. As if she did this very thing every day in Spring and summer, sat on a tractor and squinted into the sun, catching wrinkles. Her fingers rested on her thighs, her white elbow was tucked under the wheel, but she was dead so she couldn't feel how it pressed the tendon there. When Edie turned the corner on the path, her dog trotting behind her, the ghost of her mother smiled and beckoned her over. Her fingers swam in the air, her smile familiar. She patted her hair on one side, which is how Edie recognized her. But she didn't come right away, stood in the path with her dog, staring for a long second before she said, "Mother, you're dead. What are you doing here?"

Edie's mother in her gloves and hat, a little snap-catch purse on her arm, plump with health again, her horsey face with the gem-colored eyes just like Edie's holding that last light of the day, she said to Edie, "Never mind all that. Everything's all right now. I'm here."

***

By ten in the morning, the sun was hot already, though the figs outside the kitchen window moved in what must have been a breeze. Chuck had brought back bagels and upended the bag on the table. The house filled up with the smell of coffee. Edie walked out of the guest room carrying her sheets wrapped around the mattress pad, the whole bundle tucked against her chest. She stood in the hall, the bathroom door and the shower and the window in the shower behind her framing her head. She looked at me like she wanted me to ask, but I didn't. Instead I looked at her like *it's fine, whatever you need.*

"I'm sorry about the sheets. I'm bleeding," she said. "Menopause or something. Gushing. I think they call it gushing."

"It's okay, really. Don't worry about it. Do you need anything?" She shook her head. "The coffee's made, Chuck's had some. Do you want breakfast?" I took the sheets out of her arms. They were warm and heavy, like something alive. They were too heavy, really, like they'd been sopped in the tub. I was worried about Edie, there was the blood now, but it was all of it, the drinking and the way she didn't call as often, and here she'd shown up at the airport with almost no notice, without much luggage, hungry. She was pale and thin, her arms skinny and her stomach round, distended like in early pregnancy, high and tight like that. I steered her toward the coffee, promised breakfast once I'd soaked everything in cold water, and so she got a mug down, put her hand on the newspaper, turned to other things.

Downstairs, I filled the laundry tub half full, the cold rushing water drowning out whatever she and Chuck were saying to each other in the kitchen, the way they were joking, even the sound of the neighbor's dog barking. When I put the sheets in the sink, they opened like a dark-hearted tulip. The water murked up instantly. I pushed the sheets under, massaging them out of their tangle. I lost sight of my fingers in the blood billowing out every time I squeezed. Too much blood, it was like a murder. I thought it was impossible that Edie could have bled like that and wasn't unconscious, that this wasn't arterial blood, that her heart still had anything left to pump. I wondered about the walls, the floor, the mattress, I had visions of scenes from horror films, great spraying arcs of blood everywhere. I got down the upholstery cleaner just in case. When the water blackened to the color of meat stock, I drained and filled the tub again and left it to soak.

Upstairs, they'd started breakfast. I wanted to talk to Edie, so I said, "Honey, can you check the backyard? That dog—."

When he'd gone I said, "That's a lot of blood."

Edie flinched.

"Okay, just tell me. Are you hurt? Are you miscarrying?"

"I don't know, no, I'm just anemic. It's menopause. I'll see the doctor when I get back."

"You haven't yet?"

"I've been, really. It's just early menopause. You'll see." She raised an eyebrow at me as if she knew something I didn't. She sat at my breakfast table drinking coffee like it were any other morning, one hand over the top of the mug, the other on her lap. The front page was spread out on Chuck's side. She had the Living Section open to the fashions. On the stove the bacon was starting to burn.

"Edie, honestly. It's a lot of blood."

She looked at me.

"Maybe we should take you to the doctor now."

She looked over at the paper.

"Edie."

"I'll go when I get back."

She took up the newspaper and shifted in the chair, her shoulder in its silky robe turned to me, a bony, final period to the conversation. By now the bacon had burned. I put on more. Chuck came in, sniffed, said nothing, but Edie got revved up again with him there now, talked about eggs like she couldn't get enough. She was laughing at the blue jay in the window feeder who was too big and couldn't figure out how to perch, who was slopping seeds all over the ground in frustration. She took an enormous dollop of cream cheese on a plastic knife, spread it on a bagel the size of her two hands, bit it. It left a white smear on her chin, but she didn't care, she was laughing again, laughing with Chuck about the stupid, cruel shoes she'd been looking at, was going to buy, and that was when I cracked ten eggs into a bowl, added salt, pepper, dill and water, and beat them as hard as I could.

She ate them all, another bagel, and most of the bacon. Took a shower, headed into the backyard with her novel and a tall glass of orange juice. She slept there every day for the rest of the trip, suspended in the hammock that Chuck had strung up in the backyard the summer before. Into the big oak, he'd screwed a hook the size of my palm, used a chain for the fig tree, a piece thick as my wrist. He taught me to trust I wouldn't fall by holding the chain, leaning away from the tree with his whole weight on it like a water-skier holds a rope. He balanced on his heels, his back straight, tipping at a nearly forty-five degree angle. As the clouds passed across the sun, his shadow appeared, disappeared.

"See? I told you it'll hold," he said, looking over his shoulder at me standing dubious in the shade. He unrolled the hammock, hooked one eye in, then the other, smoothed it out with his hands, pulling and adjusting the ropes between the stretchers.

"Here's how you get in," he said, sitting on the edge. He swung his feet up, humping around until he lay in the center, his feet and head at the same distance from the drop of his hips. He put his hands elbow-out behind his ears and sighed heavily, a parody of relaxation, then extricated himself with what looked like a dismount. "Now you try."

I sat tentatively on the side, twisted like I imagined he had, found myself somehow horizontal. The ropes cut into the backs of my legs, the soft parts of my arms, closed almost over my hips where the stretchers didn't help. Chuck grabbed handfuls of rope, pulled toward himself like a swing, pushed it until it swayed. The light moved through the leaves and over my legs, patterns shifting, returning. When it stopped, he got a long stick, then got in the hammock with me, our two heads aligned. We lay there for a minute watching the leaves until he dropped the stick between the ropes, pushed against the ground and made the whole thing rock like a cradle.

***

The uterus is a fat, inverted pear. It has arms, they cup egg-shapes at the wrist, the fringy fingers like feathers or kelp. Around the whole are the hips, smooth and curved. Around the back, the wings of the pelvis, a bony cradle. The center of the uterus is upholstered with plush, blood-colored velvet. The margin between the emptiness at the center and this red lining is thick and soft, softer than skin. It looks like the edges of letters in old books, where the ink has bled past the pressmarks onto the pulpy paper. It looks kitten-hair soft, soft like our favorite toy as a child, like we might hug it for comfort.

And here Edie was on the phone, telling me that the doctors were planning to anesthetize her and pour boiling water into her to wash the red away, to flush her out with hot water and steam, clean out everything like janitors or laundrymen. I imagined that after the procedure, the inside would be slick and clean, a pork loin just run under the tap. I imagined standing in her womb, running my hands over the newly exposed meat, how clean and how terrible. I was in the car, she'd gone to the doctor at home, to several doctors. They'd recommended this, all of them, she said, that or a hysterectomy and she didn't want to lose everything. The highway stretched flat and straight north. It was late morning and the sun was still low enough that it scalded my arm through the window. I shifted into more shade, leaned into Chuck, listened to Edie's voice come through the static of the eight hundred miles between us.

"It's some bleeding condition. Endo-something. The gynecologist says it needs cauterizing," she said. I heard her yawn and stretch. She had just gotten out of bed.

I thought about fire irons, glowing red, pressed to dog bites. I thought screaming, writhing, thought how in movies they either died then right away, or didn't and forever had a big scar like a latex worm stuck to their skin.

"Cauterized? But why?"

"It'll remove the lining. It'll stop the bleeding."

I thought, *She'll stop having periods.*

Oh God, I thought, *No babies.*

I looked at Chuck in enough alarm that he frowned down at me, his lips forming the word, *What?*

"Edie? But what about the baby?" I caught his eye. He still didn't understand. I could see he was thinking she was miscarrying, so I put my hand over the mouthpiece. I whispered: *Surgical procedure, no baby.*

In my ear, I heard Edie laughing, but the phone made it sound as though she were standing in a room without furniture. "I can't have babies anyway, and I'm bleeding to death."

Chuck caught my eye. He mouthed: *Miscarriage?*

I shook my head, said to Edie, "But once they do that, there's no chance, you know. No endometrium, no pregnancy. They're going to sterilize you. Absolutely."

"I can't have babies anyway. And you know what? Now I'm really glad I didn't get pregnant. What would I do with a baby?" She laughed again. The sound bounced around the space between us. "I have too much work to do and no money and all this responsibility. So it's okay, really. I'm okay with this."

"Edie?" Chuck looked over at me again. I mouthed: *Operation, op. er. ay. shun.* He nodded with a million questions all over him still. I mouthed: *Later, later.* He drove on.

"No really, I'm okay with it. I didn't really want the baby anyway. And now I can stop trying and get on with things."

"Will it hurt?"

"For a couple of days," she said, "like a miscarriage."

I heard her get up for a drink. The refrigerator opened, something poured into a glass, she swallowed, then sat down on her porch, the rocking chair creaking. I heard a goldfinch singing clearly from the bed full of yellow flowers she planted every year.

When she called again a few weeks later, just a couple of days out of surgery, she talked like someone had chloroformed her, like she was sucking marbles. She told me she was lying in bed, curled up around the wound that would not stop bleeding. I could hear her rocking herself, the way the phone registered the sound of her body trying for comfort. She wanted her mother, she said, "Where is my mother? Where is my mother?"

I said, "Edie, Edie, what can I do? Let me help you, let me help you, let me call someone there," but she never heard me, she only said over and over, "It hurts, it hurts, it hurts," crying into the phone like no one was there.

***

That late at night, the neighborhood was always dark but for the few streetlamps that flicker and go out and come on again unpredictably. Ahead of me the house glowed in the darkness, every light on and the windows blazing, not stars but fires behind glass. Shadows of things passed in front of the light, looking out, moving away as I drove in. Inside, the big dog paced the great room, his tail curled and high. The dying beagle slept behind her gate in the bedroom, snoring and dreaming of food, her mouth moving around nothing. Chuck was there with the phone beside him, on the sofa, at the door, on the sofa. He was sitting me down to tell me. To tell me that Edie was dead.

I stared. How could Edie have died? Carlberg, a long-time friend of Chuck's who had worked with Edie and me, had called from Wisconsin to tell him.

"Edie's dead? Edie's dead?" I walk around the rooms, through all the rooms, repeating it, switching lights on and off. Repeating it.

"They say she killed herself."

"Edie killed herself." The kitchen light flicked on. The fluorescents sputtered and blinked. "Edie? Dead? Edie? Suicide?"

I stopped by the mantel, picked up some knick-knack. It was dusty. I thought, *Maybe I'll dust tomorrow*, knowing that would never happen.

Chuck sat down, passed the phone from one hand to the other as if it were hot.

"How is Edie dead, Chuck?" I was still holding whatever I had picked up, the vase, the iron fish, the knitting, the wooden cat, whatever it was. "How is Edie dead?"

"Sit down a minute. This is what Carlberg says. She was pregnant—"

"Now I know it's not true. She had that operation—"

"Apparently she got pregnant—"

"But if she was pregnant, she would never have—"

"No, listen for a second, okay? She got pregnant but three weeks ago she lost the baby—"

Everything above my navel squeezed so hard I thought I would never hold breath again. Not like being knocked out of a tree, but like being born.

"—lost the baby and then went on a bender, a bad one. Ended up in the hospital."

"Hospital. Edie's dead in the hospital."

"No, listen. She's dead at home, or probably now at the funeral home, actually, fuck I don't know where she's dead now, but she killed herself at home."

I could only look at the floor. I sat down. The dog stood beside me but watched the front windows in case something moved. I petted him shamelessly, his ears, each one, his neck ruff, all the way down to his tail, each leg, his belly, hairy, then bare. He shivered in pleasure. I stopped.

"Carlberg says she checked herself out of the hospital, got a gun, and took pills and shot herself. Her boyfriend found her yesterday sometime."

"She didn't shoot herself."

"I don't know, but that's what Carlberg says."

"She didn't have a gun. She didn't like guns. Shoot herself. She didn't. I know she didn't."

"What can I do? I feel terrible. I've known for hours and couldn't tell you. Are you okay? What can I do?"

"She didn't shoot herself," I said, "she didn't she didn't," like a child, crying against what emphatically is. What I knew was the truth, once the calls started coming late into the night, everyone hollow on the line, in other rooms, at other times. And when I became too tired to fight it finally, sitting waiting for the phone to ring again after midnight after so much talking and so much left to do, I saw in my mind the basement of her house in Madison, with that big double bed, piled with blankets, comforters, afghans. I saw the curtain across the way to the washer, how Mr. Jones, Edie's cat, lived down there in the cool. I saw the back of the china chest at the foot of the bed, I saw it outlining the lumps of my feet and Chuck's feet under the covers, a human landscape against the back of the china chest in which she kept things she loved, and which I'd given her for her wedding because she'd always wanted it. And here it was in my mind again.

I put Edie on the floor beside it. I put the gun to her head and watched it go off in a kind of movie slow motion, her head recoiling, what was left of it. I watched in my mind how the bits of bone and brain made a spray pattern on the wood, maple if I remembered correctly, with fake gilding and trimwork touched in aging red paint. I forgot Edie slumping on the floor to study the blood on the wood: not Jackson Pollack, who would seem the most straightforward comparison, but something more focused and deliberate and monochromatic. I thought about the way hoses work water into this pattern, if the spray nozzle is right. Except unlike paint, water's so ephemeral. Blood seeps. I thought, *It seeps*.

I put the phone on the floor near Edie's body, with the pill bottle picturesquely arranged near her right hand (brown bottle, white cap, a few missed sea-foam green pills rolled to the lowest point near her right knee). I put the phone there because I wanted her to want someone to call and to hope for it.

The next morning, I woke up half-dreaming, thinking, *Edie is dead*, imagining her body instead now far from her phone, so far it looked like it was at the end of a tunnel, at the wrong end of a telescope. Unreachable. I imagined this time that she'd shot herself in the bathroom rather than the basement, to contain the mess, and had not aimed at her head at all, but at her heart. Not knowing guns well, she'd missed, shot her arm or her stomach or her leg. The gun lay beside the tub, between it and the toilet. Her hand rested beside it, a little bloody (not much since it's mostly draining into the tub), her hand with its beautiful sapphires in platinum, with its long languid druggy fingers, the long arm, the shoulder with its freckles, Edie, her face pale, her eyes like mountain lakes in midsummer, that blue, that vacant, and all she wants is someone to help her, but no one's there. She's wearing dangling earrings that rest on her neck where there's still a pulse. Her glasses are on the back of the toilet with the empty pill bottle. The tub smells faintly of rose salt scrub and lavender and Ivory soap. Her washcloth dangles, slightly damp, from a hook under the window and her elbow's pressing the side of the tub in a way that reminds her of when she was small and her mother let her play in the bath like it was the ocean. Her chest rises, falls, the phone's downstairs, through the mirror, and she's thinking now she might have waited an hour or two, or a day or two or a whole lifetime or two, but no one's coming and she can't reach the phone and as she dies she wants to more and more until it's the last thought she has: *I have to call someone.*

In my mind, in this vision I have, the last thing I imagine is Edie's phone beginning to ring downstairs. The way the answering machine picks it up, the way Edie's voice comes on to ask for a message, the way whoever it is who's calling throws that message into the air like a fish hook towards the sea, all its potential hanging at the top of that curve of motion, right before it comes down.

Paradise

Chorus angelorum tu suscipiat
—In Paradisum, Requiem mass

The high school choir director looks over his shoulder, his face bunched tightly around his nose, his mustache a little brown brush underneath. He rakes it with his teeth, huffs it out again. "No one's making you do this," he says.

"Okay," I say, shoving my back into the practice room wall, squaring my shoulders like I'm good for it, game for it. I'm fifteen, a sophomore in high school. My books are slung into my crossed arms loosely, the spiral wires on my notebook make pressure-patterns on my skin. I don't own a bookbag, and Trapper Keepers are years off. I put the books on a chair and shut the heavy door. It locks automatically. Into that silence, the air conditioner rattles on.

Mr. Richards plays a note on the upright piano that bulks up the room, a mountain fitted into a box. It's just the two of us and that huge instrument. The note he plays sits under my left lung and hums there. He plays the note again, lets it hang, watches me over his shoulder through his bronze-tinted glasses. "Sing," he says.

I feel it tingle, that note. I hum it, move it upwards to my throat, upwards to my sinuses, open my mouth and release it. The sound I make, icy and precise, buzzes the walls and the floor, lingers in the sympathetic wires of the piano humming back at me friendly-like, sotto voce, nearly unhearable. Mr. Richards plays the note again. "Do that again," he says. This time, the sound flies fast out between my eyes and slices into the wall just over his head. He plays another note, a series of them. I lean into the sound I make. I embody it like a spigot embodies water.

At the bottom of my range, the notes sit in my knees, in an elbow, under my left arm. They clot and darken and then refuse to leave. I don't so much go silent as shut down. Mr. Richards shifts to his right. "Okay," he says, "try this one." It pings a cheekbone and I pigeon it into the air. I sing the next notes and the next ones, peeling the ceiling away and filling the sky, the whole sky and everything above it. The last note Mr. Richards plays finds no place in my body, ghosts me entirely on its way elsewhere. He turns on the bench to face me. "You'll be an alto," he says. I don't know what an alto is. I say, "I'm in the choir?" There is a look on his face that says I haven't been listening. "Yes. You're in the choir."

***

We are practicing in the side-aisle of a cathedral in some small English town, and though it is high summer, the air is clotted-cold. Our voices break against the stone pillars, against the stone walls and floor. We stamp our feet, start again. "Who are you standing on?" the woman next to me whispers. We're on our college choir tour, four countries in three weeks. "Eleanor," I say. "Eleanor someone, I can't see for sure." I have never sung on top of a grave, never stood in a church cram-full of dead bodies. I try not to step on Eleanor's face, her chest, any part of her. It's impossible. The director clears his throat; the choirmaster hums the A; we pick up the first note of our parts. I see the chord appear, a reddish-pink haze hanging just above us.

The sopranos begin, we altos come in two or three measures after, then the tenors arrive, high in their registers. The song begins to appear, I begin to taste the music—licorice, coffee, smoky and rich, buttered toast a little burned. Comes a cadence, the building breathes our voices back to us, stone and glass and all the bones we stand on. We settle into the next number, tourists stopping to listen, to look at the light tumbling through the windows, to read the gravestones they're walking on, their necks craning down, craning up.

I have an apple in my bag for later, and after practice we all find the sun outside. It's the same light that had risen through the glass over the altar and lit up the face of Jesus—the little lambs gamboling, the green grass his feet don't quite touch. We fall onto the actual grass around the building in various postures of rest, lying between the headstones and under the yews. I read the markers aloud, pick a Margaret because that was my grandmother's name, press into her body-warm headstone like lying against my mother's shoulder.

***

In Wisconsin, where I move for work, a former student who needs to teach voice for his degree decides to give me lessons. We meet at a local church he's borrowed for a Saturday. "I'm a low voice," I say, doing my best low-voice impression. Ken stares at me a moment: "I'm a vocal educator. We'll see." His voice fills the space, rising to the rafters, resting about forty feet above us against the wooden beams of the nave. I open my mouth and sing the A I know by heart by then, every tuning-A at every concert. It's a bird chucked into the sky to test the weather. I say the C above it, then the G above that, the A lost before the chord flickers into being, though I can hear it like a shadow. Ken plays it on the piano. He pedals it to keep it there, I sing the G again, move it a half step down and feel the dissonance in my elbows and knees.

I stand in the very center of the room, my head turned up a little. We do scales from there. The higher we go, the more yellow I see, the more the air fills with minnows, blue-green and silver flashes. At some point, everything explodes in light. The windows are on fire, a thousand tiny lamps. They feed the notes back to me in their colors, a perfect pink, a hand-painted gold, the roof dripping with what I've sung just before. I lift a handful of sound and fling it into the air, over and over again. We pass over the shift to head voice, Ken marking it on a sheet of paper. We go and go, it's electric behind my cheekbones, electric in my ears, pitches so high I feel like I'm beckoning pure white dogs that fly. Ken stops. I stop. I take a drink of water.

"Tenor my butt," he says. He plays ten notes. I recognize it as the higher part of the Queen of the Night's aria. "Sing that." I had never thought to. I open my mouth. The notes are ten drops of mercury. I touch them, each one. I repeat this until the mercury spots are themselves but also a rivulet of silver running over glass. "Tenor," he says, "my butt."

"Do you like singing the melody?" Ken asks. I don't know. As an alto, I almost never sang it in a choir. In a choir, altos are richness, the egg yolk underneath, almost never the main anything. It suited me. I didn't know if I would like the melody. "Too bad," Ken says, "because that?" He taps my throat, right where the hard part is. "That will destroy people."

We close the piano, collect our things, lock the door. The snow lies in big dirty humps up against the walls of the church. I stand for a minute, envision myself in a Queen of the Night get-up, witchy, painted, big as Godzilla stomping people. I am singing, flinging people with my voice against buildings in some operatic reproduction of New York. I spot the Met and stomp toward it. I am destroying with my voice. "Lord no, that's never me," I say to the back of Ken's jacket. "That's never me."

***

Chuck and I play tennis late at night, the coolest part of a summer day. We try to avoid sucking in mayflies, but they're thick as oats, every swing of the racket cuts them down. I don't understand tennis, but he has played it all his life, an early athlete. He sets me behind the back line, stands over on his side, throws the ball gently across the net. I hit it. It travels past him, many feet over his head. He comes over, adjusts the racket in my hand, kisses my neck. I giggle, wait for him to throw the next one, shifting foot to foot like I've seen on TV. He tosses it, a little arc of green. I hit it hard, fast, so fast it surprises him into not getting out of the way. The ball smacks the meat of his thigh. The next throw I pound too, jamming the whole Spring-shot contraption of my body into it. The ball blasts into the chain-link far outside the box to his right. He lowers the net. Repositions the racket. Tries to show me how to aim. It's wasted, I can't. The ball shoots away every time, left, right, over, sometimes into the box, usually not.

It's past midnight, the walk is not long back down the street to the house I'd bought the year before, before I knew him. Lying in bed I say, "Well, I can't play tennis." He snorts, his hand on my heart. "But I can sing," I say, "I can sing you straight to sleep." I brush the hair back from his freckled forehead, an inversion of the night sky. He settles against his pillow against my shoulder, blind without his glasses, everything a blur of night, my face a pale punctuated moon. Outside the stars are wheeling into the morning. I sing, *Oh very young, what will you leave us this time?* but that's the only lyric I know to that song, so I switch over to a Christmas carol, then a song I sang as a child. He is not asleep. "I used to direct the Navy choir," he says to the moon. "It was easier than doing boot camp and no one wanted it." Later I hear him downstairs making coffee in the kitchen, me curled into a knot still, reluctant to get up.

Finally I roll over and stretch, half-awake, feeling the way my muscles ache, then the heaviness of my abdomen suddenly. It clutches, wired and tense and zinging. I frown, wondering, touch myself under my boxers. My hand comes up sticky with blood. I stand up, catch myself against the wall, don't catch myself against the wall. Suddenly there is blood everywhere, on the wall, my hands, under me. I didn't know there could be so much, so thick with the baby I didn't know I was losing. Lying on the floor, I cry out, *Chuck Chuck*, projecting to the balconies, a trick Ken taught me.

***

Soon afterwards, Chuck and I move elsewhere, but there is no work for me and the babies we make die and die. I stop singing entirely, stop speaking when my husband's not there and sometimes when he is. I lie in bed instead in our new house, or walk to the store and buy nothing, or sit on the seawall down at the bay staring at the sea grass. Once in a while I see a dolphin, its gray back scarred white all over. Sometimes it rolls its eye up and I see it wondering, this life, that life, how to live in one, breathe in another.

I don't remember how I find the Chalifouxs or why, but one indefinite day Chuck and I are in the car, and he says, "They're good teachers, and you can sing again." He is holding my hand, his thumb rubbing a tender bit of my wrist. I say nothing, the highway out the window an elaborate tangle of concrete veins impossible to understand except from airplanes. "If you want to sing again," he says. "I mean, no one is making you do this." We pull up in the driveway of a stuccoed single-story house surrounded by masses of indiscriminate green. I squint at them, thinking their names: Podocarpus, lantana, dracaena. Everything named, everything safe. I open my door, collect my water bottle, my batch of music—some art songs Ken once gave me, a photocopy of Bach's *Magnificat*, a Stabat Mater someone thought would suit me.

"I'm not sure I can do this," I say.

"I know," he says. "If you can't, just call me and I'll come pick you up."

There's a grand piano in their living room, some upholstered chairs, a stereo system in an inexpensive shelving unit. On other shelves sit pieces of china, books, silk plants—philodendron, phalaenopsis, athyrium. Timothy introduces himself and his wife, a Lithuanian woman, Clementina. She has warm hands but discerning eyes. "Have you brought something to sing?" she says. I hand Timothy the Stabat; he sits at the piano and rummages through the accompaniment. A tiny Italian greyhound named Puck joins us. The dog licks a place on my leg, a mosquito bite I cannot stop scratching. It wells blood even now. The dog licks and sniffs, licks and sniffs. I reach down to stroke his head, flexible ears attached to a silk-covered tennis ball extending into a delicate snout.

I say to Puck, "I haven't sung now in many years and I'm not sure I can anymore and I have really no clear idea what I'm doing here except wasting your time, I'm so sorry, please forgive me, really." I find I can't breathe, that sentence longer than any I've spoken in I don't know how long. I am miserable, about to cry.

They look quizzical. "Well," Clementina says, "we shall see and decide whether the instrument is pretty enough to bother." Her hair is a beautiful fall of silver, held back by a single mother-of-pearl clip above her ear, the hair thick though she is certainly well into her 70s. Her face she arranges into cold objectivity. She looks past me and waits, ready to judge.

Timothy plays the first few bars of the second movement, the soprano singing alone. I stand silent, unable to sing, wondering why I've chosen the Stabat. It's so unfamiliar, I've never sung it more than for warming up. Timothy helpfully plays just the first note of the solo, a beautiful vibrating note right in my range, a note I am too unnerved to identify and in any case it dies, absorbed by the carpet, the books, the walls with their smooth gray paint. Timothy plays the note again, using the damper to extend the sound. But I can hear nothing, nothing lingers, nothing lives. Even the dog is sleeping now, under a table, unmoved. "I can't do this," I say. "Please."

Clementina listens to the note die. "No one can make you sing," she says. "What did you come here to do?"

I see over her shoulder the blue of their pool, its aureole of concrete, the open sky above the cage that keeps out the leaves and dirt. I say, "Can I sing out there?" She gets up, Timothy stays at his piano. She opens a wall of sliders under the concrete outdoor overhang that protects a small patio from the rain. The floor is big ceramic tiles. Our steps change—they sound and bounce. I say, "Here. Is it okay here?"

She is closing the glass doors when I hear the A in the snick of them in their tracks, clear as a voice calling over a mountain—*Over here, I've found something*. I sing that A into the glass doors that give it back to me in all its shuddering tenuousness. I can hear how dusty I sound, how the sadness has collected in my throat and head. When I lean into and out of the A, I see dark brown hares, they scatter, escaping into dense yarrow hedges, hares shifting their shoulders through the green. As I sing, their racing becomes not scattering but choreography, a spirograph, lines that linger.

The note I sing ends in the air over the pool behind me, dropping out into the water itself. I sing a verse of "Shenandoah," then a hymn I learned at college, then a Christmas carol, then the first few bars of the Stabat Mater soprano solo. It feels like moving my legs after sitting all day, tender, full of work. The colors come in ochre, the green of leaflitter, the batter-color of a moon rising at the horizon. They flicker, a bad film on too slow a speed. I stop. "I haven't sung in so long," I say. "I'm so sorry to waste your time. I have no idea what I'm doing here at all."

"Well," Clementina says. Her hand rests on the door pull, each nail sharpened to a point and lacquered. I blush deep red. Timothy stands behind the sliders with Puck beside him, both just gray shapes against the glass. My reflection looks faded, the bright hot light behind me, the aqua-blue of the pool, the crayon green of the lawn behind it. "We will be happy to teach you," she says.

***

My husband says, the week before he dies, that he will sing for me one day. He promises. We are lying in bed, his head on my stomach. He says, "I have never felt like I could, not with you." I run my fingers through his hair, his long, cloud-gray hair. "Shh," I say, "there's time. Some day. Maybe you'll feel like singing to our boy when he gets here." We're adopting, our son coming in just four months, we learn that day—a dozen years and a dozen or more dead babies later. My husband puts a hand under my leg, squeezes and says nothing, not then and never again anything about singing.

***

Clementina sits in her chair facing the piano and me, my back to Timothy. "Today," she says, "we will practice through the break." This is the hardest thing I know, to sing the notes in the shift between chest and head voice. We start just with long-held notes. In this dead room, they are dead, but I am not listening so much as trusting Clementina to listen. I am instead doing body work, placing the note in parts of my head, shoveling air over my vocal cords with my intercostals and abdominal muscles, ignoring my throat entirely since it's really just a window in the room of sound, open or closed this much, that much, automated by musculature I don't have to pay attention to right now. I don't see anything when I work this way but the parts of my body I want to engage: my skull the skin of a drum, the strapping of muscles in my torso, thick and red as raw steaks, the fisty joints at my hips and knees, the ligaments tense or loosened. Each adjustment I make shifts the sound around my body, around the air around my body, into the world. The notes I sing sour, turn rich and fuzzy, are too sharp, flat, wrong. Then, once or twice for a moment, electrically right. I stop. I apologize.

Timothy says, "We think it's time you auditioned."

Audition. I can't.

"I'd rather just practice."

Clementina frowns again, her tannin-colored irises visible even when she narrows her eyes in annoyance. "Stand up straight, do not let your chest pull you into a curl. Now," she recrosses her ankles and adjusts a fold of her pants. "It's a choir, you see, and you should be heard, but a choir, this makes sense to us. With your reticence."

A choir. I could do a choir. I think.

Chuck lights up when I mention it, so I commit. My teachers and I pick an easy piece placed high in my range but not stratospherically so. We practice, I practice at home, I get so I am singing it everywhere in the house, in the garden, as I pace out the day, everywhere. But when I hand the sweat-damp music to the choir mistress at the audition in a local church, I discover I've forgotten it. The pianist shoves his glasses up his nose and waits. I wait. He plays a note. "Sing this."

The sound I make is tentative, light. I adjust my feet, and try again, I say the note, which I realize is a G, a G the color of summer ferns—a little darker, a little curlier and fringed, than fiddleheads in Spring. I unfurl it into the space of this church the way watercolor infuses a wet page. Into the most intense light of an afternoon, which is nowhere but in my mind, the fronds spread themselves. I see a day on the moors near Lake Windemere, my husband striding up a rise, and the shape of him against the sky, a ship in a froth of ferny green wake. I breathe.

The choir mistress crosses her arms, says to the pianist: "Play 'God Save the Queen.'" To me: "Do you know that one?" I nod. "Sing."

It is the easiest singing I ever do. This is "My Country 'Tis of Thee," and I see suddenly that I am standing again in the fourth grade, my hand over the general region of my heart under the plaid pin-tucked bodice of a dress, out of which stick my too-long, scabby legs. I want to scratch my hair full of the itch of sand from falling off the monkey bars into the dirt before school. I open my mouth instead and sing, *God save our gracious queen long live our glorious queen god save the queen*, but it's really *My country 'tis of thee sweet land of liberty to thee I sing*. All around me the little terrible voices of children with no idea what we're singing, but we're singing anyway, our sticky hands over our hearts and recess is coming soon with its release, we know. And there the song ends, and we shuffle into our desks. What I see has the smell of heat and old wood, it has the feel of spelling lessons, it is so familiar I am erased in the moment, just the body with the voice that sings *God save the queen! (Let freedom ring!)*.

"You've sung in choirs before." I nod. "You know how to blend?" I nod, blending is what I do.

I say, "I sang alto for most of my life. Or tenor."

"Do you want to sing alto?" the choir mistress says. I want to be useful, but I like the high notes, the way they shatter and color things. I shake my head. "Soprano it is, up with the rest of them, then." I am in the choir, our next performance is Fauré's Requiem, three months from now. My teachers applaud when I tell them, Timothy beaming, Clementina compressing her lips with happiness. Chuck holds me, takes me to Home Depot to distract me with buying flowers and pavers, hopeful.

***

The week after Chuck dies, my mother says, "Does it help to imagine him waiting for you in heaven?" She says, "God has a plan for you, this is part of that plan."

I say, "There is no plan nor any god, Mom. There is only this."

We are silent a moment, listening to the old dog lap water from his dish.

She says, "When I dream, I don't dream about your father. I dream about my mother, it's always my mother. She's the only one I want to see when I die."

I say, holding my own hand, "Help me, Mom. Please, I don't know how to do this."

She pats my shoulder, stares at the wall in front of us. We sit there on the sofa, listen while the dog paces and grunts as he lies down again, as it gets darker. At last she falls asleep next to me, her mouth open, her chest barely rising. I walk to the place in the house where he died, curl up on the floor just there and rest one hand where I imagine his heart was and stopped, and wait.

***

The countertenor's F-sharp is clear-toned, a little boy's voice in an empty room. It calls out over the audience in their pews, across the transept and into the rose window, which pitches it, an echo, back down the nave. The singer holds his note too long, a sostenuto not marked in the score. We in the choir attend, the conductor's arms embracing air, eyebrows lifted so that we're ready to move on when the soloist releases. We steady ourselves, holding our D *sempre dolce*, the sound of what we're wishing for: angels' wings, our mother's voices whispering good morning, our waking up in paradise sweet and eager as children. The countertenor's note is a depthless white, an icicle on the tongue.

The audience waits with us, rapt, silent. My mother sits near the middle, Chuck holding her hand. The organist in his loft stills his restless, high arpeggios, his pedaling too, a heartbeat paused for that moment.

A Remembrance of Things Past Remembering

I discover my mother in a rehabilitation hospital packing her things, only these are not her things, these are trash things, used diapers, plastic wrap, wads of Kleenex, her purse turned inside out, her incomprehension, memories of her mother, desire for her mother, the way her mother touched her face as a girl and forgave her, the way the kitten felt wiggly and soft when she brought it home in her pocket, the dancing she did in the basement, the smell of her aunts' cooking, how they said *potatoes* in that lilting Irish as they peeled them, the sound of the pieces hitting the pan, the taste of the raw peel they gave her, the feel of their legs against her ear and the thick nobs of their knees against her cheek, the sight of her father walking in the door, the way he rolled his ankles when he walked, her mother's fingers in her hair, loosening her braids, her mother's kiss before sleeping, the doll she pressed to her neck, the unrolling dream of the roads rivering up into the blue mountains outside town

The sack in her hand in the hospital room is transparent, with white handles that click together to close tightly, but her arm is dipping in and out, her hand scouring the reefs, and once when we were underwater, she turned to me, the regulator in her mouth making that sucking-bubbling sound, her eyes were so magnified I thought they would take up her whole face, and she shifted her head back to look up at the surface, at the blot of the sun blazing behind the mirror of the surface (up where she could not be suffocated in water), which is exactly a gesture she made the last time I saw her, in her wheelchair, trying to catch her breath, trying to make the cage of her ribs let her bird-heart go, or rather to keep it there, or something—because it's not at all clear anymore what she wants to do, where she wants to be, how she wants to live, if she wants to live here where mostly she stays behind her closed eyes and sometimes, surely, she has to feel crushed under all this needing to keep her heart plodding down this road on its tired flat feet with both soles loose at all the seams

Her hand in the sack digs in the dirty diapers, pushing everything wet aside, she says my name, she says "Emily, Emily—Emily is in here, can you help me, she is in here," and how am I in there and in her mind too? Her hand snouts around for me in her own waste and worry and this is when

I become a memory that will not be retained, which is not me, not what I am to her—there among what will end up in a landfill, like the both of us, which is, I stand there thinking, exactly what should happen, that she is a fool, that she is telling a truth, we are (ridiculous) this tissue, that lipstick

She says: "Shh they are trying to kill me," and I can't think who would try to kill this old woman in her paper pants wet to the knees, which must be cold, which must be clammy, and her paper shirt that is like the bag around her hand and just barely holds her inside it, there are ties at the neck, the sleeves bell, her dress at her wedding had so many pearl buttons it took, she once said to me with her hand just going all crooked in the joints, crooked around the bell of the wine glass mostly full of something white and cold and bitter, about an hour to fasten her in, buttons up the wrists, buttons up the back and over a corset she didn't need, the waist at twenty inches, the bust full with tulle to give her breasts she didn't have yet, though she was twenty-two when they married at the local church, her sisters in the wedding, "All those buttons," she said to me, breathing out something between acetone and grape juice, they took it all off her to put her into something my father could ease her out of the night of their wedding and with this she looks away out the window like the past is there

"They are trying to kill me, I don't like this hotel, there's a parade in the hall but they are trying to kill me," she insists, then sits on the bed, her bag of trash beside her, so I sit down beside her and I say, "Mom, here is some candy, let's have a piece of that together," and I unwrap a piece of something chocolate that she tucks into the bag for later, as if there's a later she will understand as later, not the eternal now in which she, like any quivering creature, is hunted, cornered, and slaughtered just for living, just for (she imagines, I imagine) being, and so I say, "Mom, can we change your pants do you think" and she looks at me and says, "Emily, you fuss too much, there is no reason to change and anyway no time since Father is here and he needs me to get on my shoes, but I can't find the left one and the car is waiting," so she looks at me with those eyes that are not the eyes I have looked into all my life and I am not me, I am not there, we are not here, we are not sitting together on a hospital bed in a rehabilitation facility with a bag of trash for packing and now she is crying, wailing, the tears a complete mask that splotch the blue paper over her breasts a darker blue and all of the sudden she says, "Emily, Emily, where are we, what happened, did I hit my head? Is this the hospital"

"It's Mother's Day," I say, "should we change pants and go out to dinner?" and I have been pressing the bell for a nurse, trying to get someone to change her and put her in a shower and instead the television is shouting something about the weather and my mother hisses, "Go away go away go away you don't get to see me like this" and with all her might she shoves herself out of the bed leaping for the door with her bag of trash that holds me in it and she is in the hall before I can recall her to herself as if I could call her anywhere, trapped as I am in this locked bathroom, trapped because something has happened and I can't get out "Mom Mom Mom," I call, but she is sleeping or gone and so I figure out how to jimmy the lock and maybe she never was where I thought she was which is the most likely thing you can imagine, I think, when the orderly who is so kind rolls up with a chair for my mother, he is young and handsome and my mother thinks he's the maid, so he plays the maid for her, listens to her complain about the service, ask about checking out, what she owes, and I say, "Can she shower and change? and can you get someone to help her and get her fresh?"—I wave an arm that folds in the whole world

She is clean, in pajamas, she smells of powder and lotion like a soft baby. I hand her the phone and she explains that I have taken her out to dinner at a restaurant she can't remember the name of and that her whole family is there, of course, making sure she is remembered and she's ordered the biggest steak and "Shh," she says to me, "You can't say that I'm lying because this is a white lie, it makes people feel better that you don't want to be with them, so you say I'm sick or I have other plans, and everyone knows this is a white lie," but I say, "Mom, don't you want to play bridge with Mrs. Peres?" and she says, "No, not really" (she is smoking, her bouffant enormous and flipped at the ends), "I would rather stay here," she says as she sips her drink and looks over the rim at me, her hand around the martini she's made for herself, "It's a white lie, a white lie," and when she hands me the phone my brother says: "You're at the rehab, right? Not at a restaurant, no steak, nothing like that," and I say, "Yes," but I know that what she said is not a lie, she is not lying now, everything else was a lie, the forgetting, the panic, this facility, the crawling to the finish line, but this, this here, this Mother's Day dinner she believes in and sees is not a lie at all, and she tastes this steak even though it's ice cream she's cutting with a little plastic knife and lifting to her mouth to chew.

Wonderland

It wasn't at all what I had imagined all my life. Not the people in it, not the setting, not anything. It was so different that I can hardly remember what I believed about meeting my birthmother for so long, only that in my mind, she would be dark and large as I had been told she was, more like a grandmother than a mother. She would wear something flowered and bright-colored, she would have warm hands, strong and large and puffed with sweetness like doughnuts or sugary baked goods. She would wear one narrow gold band grown too small for her finger after many years of marriage to another man, not the man who made me, someone who was willing to be my father but who wasn't really, who had kind dark eyes that saw me as someone nice by negligible. Not his, hers; and not really hers either. We would meet in a kitchen somewhere—her house, my house—and she would hug me. And then we would sit down and talk at the table, talk about how it was for her. She would be happy and smile my smile at me, a confirmation.

My imaginings never went beyond this one meeting, so I am at a loss for all the days that followed the one on which I met her, I met a them that I never anticipated. What I imagined was a Hollywood creation, a stereotypical scene fit for drama in half-hour segments. Not real life, never real—I know that now, knowing its antithesis. It could never have been the way I imagined it at all, never. And it wasn't.

***

Anna, my birthmother, did not want me to come to California, to have to be among so many new faces at first, to startle me away with strangers. Nor did she want to come to Wisconsin, afraid as she was to meet me without familiar places to hide in, out in the open where she might be exposed. In the end, I think she was afraid of what she might find when she came; afraid of who I might be and what I might think of her.

So, though she said on the phone that Tuesday afternoon when we spoke for the first time that she would see me soon, she postponed and postponed. Instead of my parents, I got phone calls and email telling me it would be too much to come, too overwhelming. Instead of coming, she said she would wait.

Then one day, my birthfather Joe told me, he came home, his feet swarmed by the foster dogs and puppies she collected, his hands full of briefcase and sunglasses, to discover that she was ready. She had bought plane tickets and they were going to see me after all, and soon. She had done it while he was at work, decided and planned it, so he looked into hotels, found the Pfister, and booked a suite for a long weekend: two rooms, one to sleep in, one to meet me in. Then he wrote to say that they would be there in Milwaukee in a few days—there not fifty miles from me, within driving distance, the two people who had made me, whom I never knew, whom I was about to know.

And so I began imagining this version of that meeting, how I would pick them up at the airport and take them to the hotel. How I would bring them flowers and gifts. How they wouldn't know what to say, and I wouldn't know what do to with my hands. And they wouldn't know what to do with theirs either, but needing to find their bags, needing to get into the car, having to drive—I would have work to do to distract me. I would not have to make conversation about us, or the thirty-five missing years, or try to figure out what to say to strangers who are also family. Instead: finding, lifting, packing, driving, moving. It would be a comfort.

But this too was not what happened. Joe writes to say they would prefer to meet me at the hotel, in their room. So I find that I have to drive to the hotel, walk into it and use an elevator, walk down a hotel hall, and knock on a door in order to find them. I have to do all this with a face that has only the task of negotiating space, with hands that have only button-pressing and clenching and knocking to do, with feet that have nothing to do but walk those steps. Stand. Walk. Instead, I have nothing to do but do it, and I find I am nearly incapable of it. It's not enough.

And yet when I come to their door that night, I find I've done it, and could do it, and am amazed at it all, that I can.

***

It would, of course, have to happen in a snowstorm.

I learned to drive in snow just that year, only because I could no longer avoid knowing how to, only because my boyfriend was going away to

Princeton and I would have to make the eight or nine miles between my new house and my office on my own, as I had to do everything else. I knew to wait out the snowfall, to drive, if it were possible, after everything had been shaken out of the dark clouds, after trucks had poured beige grit and salt on it, melted and uncongealed it, made rain of it and not ice. I knew to drive slowly, to avoid curves and braking. I knew all this, and yet. I can drive in hurricane winds and torrential downpours, I can drive for hours anywhere, but this was almost too much. On this night when everything is a portent of everything else, there is snow too.

It was the perfect metaphor, the perfect atmosphere, for what I was doing. In the Midwest, before it snows, the sky lowers, darkens and closes, the air feels compressed, dangerous, electric, the darkness thick. To drive to Milwaukee that night, I got into my small white car, small as a snowflake itself, and me in the black part on the inside, black-clothed and dark-haired, heavy, grave, expectant. To get to Milwaukee, I drive a black path with white all around it and gray streaks into a gray sky. Just a few weeks ago the sky was deep blue curved over green grass, over Queen Anne's lace and flowering chicory, and I wished this path were a summer one, easier, less fraught. As I drove, the white of the car, the white of the curbs, this white came out of the sky too, and all was whiteness, all became that streaky whiteness with gray in between, nothing differentiated. I drove into this obscurity, into this miasma, an obscurity and miasma myself, the yellow lines to guide me lost in blowing snow. I thought on the way how easy it would be to aim the car off the road, to be adrift forever in the snow, to be hidden and safe and enclosed, to creep slowly into a cold sleeping death with all those people rushing by and not stopping, not knowing to stop. Never to be different, never to be anything else, not to be seen again until Spring. Covered and safe until the heat came, the green and the sky blue as cobalt glass, the sun suspended glowing in it.

But I didn't drive into the ditches. I didn't slide or hit someone or something. I drove until I found my exit. I exited and drove until I found the hotel. I parked in the pay lot, my body knotted with trying to see, my hands sore with holding on, white and pink with cold. My breath coming like a runner's, a spume of it into the iciness, the snow falling over me like a cloak covering me with the whiteness of that night, with the frozen ashes the sky shook out to make me gray.

***

I was late. I am often late. I was late this time by several minutes, though I had planned to be early. The snow and the cold delayed me, the carefulness they necessitated. When I got to the hotel, I called Joe to say I was there, waiting, despite the snow. I had imagined them in their rooms expecting the phone to ring in an agony of restlessness, wondering if I would come at all.

I said, "I am here in the lobby. Will you come down?"

I thought, here in this lobby at least there are other people, here at least it is neutral ground, here among the paintings and dark statues and lurid gilding.

But I am told I must go to them, must wait, then go to them. Unexpected.

Joe says into the phone—my God, into a phone whose cord is only a few hundred feet long, and I think, *If I just pull hard he will come to me through this wall, down through the floors and into this one, and there is just this cord here and my hand wrapping and wrapping in it, I could just—*

He says, "Can we have a little time? Say nine o'clock?"

I think, *It's a trap.* I think, *I've come and they won't see me. I'll be here all night, waiting, but they will not open the door one crack and let me in. It'll be as it always was, full of a particular rejection.* I think, *Unendurable, not again.* I think, *I must be safe, I must not let this happen.* I think, *I must not be—*

I say, "Sure, that's fine. Are you positive it's enough time?"

I think, *Surely it's enough, too much. It's thirty-six years of not knowing, it's enough time, and he will say it is enough,* and I think, *I must not cry I must not cry now I must not.* And I think, *I have parents and I don't need these and they will go no matter what anyway because they have before and it will not be enough time, there will not be enough time until they are dead or I am and then it will be plenty. Then there will be enough time to—*

"Yes," he says.

I think, *Should I say, "We can wait until morning"? Should I say, "You know, we don't have to do this"?* There's something in me that wants to, that wants to offer anything to keep from having to meet them. I knew they would shut the door once they saw me, a reflex they would have as genuine and as untaught and as unthought as the sudden involuntary snatching back of the hand from a hot surface. And then I would have to do the same but bigger, a rejection that encompassed all of us. And I think, after all, having given me away once, wouldn't the second time be most natural, most comfortable, most right? Wasn't it not only possible but probable that they would go away, never in my life, now completely out of it?

I say, "Nine. Yes. I'll be there."

And so we hang up the phone and wait again, forty minutes is no time really, only forty minutes after thirty-six years, who can mind that? Only a little more than a television program, a little less than the time I spend in the pool three mornings a week. Forty minutes, and I sit on the bed in the room I took in case I could not get home that night, I sit watching the red numbers on the clock face shift almost imperceptibly one into the other, change not cataclysmic, just a matter of one light switching off and one on sometimes, I sit watching the time pass so slowly, too slowly on the thing that measures and therefore makes it.

***

The hallway is pinky gray-white, the color of my arm in this winter, a dead color, a non-color. The walls are wainscoted, then painted this color, and there are lights on sconces sticking out at regular intervals casting cones of warm yellow incandescence on a carpet with a short, smooth nap and an unobtrusive pattern. This hallway does what all hallways in all old buildings do, meanders left and right, has unexpected changes in level, steps that disappear in the pattern of the carpet that trip you up. It's a hallway with the personality of an old man who fishes and drinks and scandalizes, pees in dark corners, rambles off into the woods, talking, laughing to himself. It's a hallway in which so many have lost themselves that the front desk provides its patrons with a map, a real map on paper. When I ask for one, the concierge turns it right side up to me across the desk, then makes a black X where my parents are.

Thus it becomes a treasure map, this paper, and I find I must negotiate all the hazards such things describe. There are elevators to choose, floors to punch, spirals and convolutions of hall, deep and round as shells, and I turn back and turn back on myself, passing what look like the same elevators, the same doors, the same potted palms. It's an illusion, though; I am really getting somewhere. I know this only at the end, only because I finally get there, to the door of their room. I don't remember the number, I don't remember anything about that door though I stood there I can't say how long, straining for their voices and not hearing them, feeling— since their door was at the end of a stretch of hall angled acutely like an elbow and sloped gently down—like I was Alice tumbling down a rabbit hole and all perspective was shifting, changing. Eat me drink me not requisite, only be me. And here was the door, and here was the risk and the door all made one.

And here at the end of the hall is the door and there is breathing and a rushing sound like wings and I find these are mine, my heart and my lungs come into my ears. There is a hand, too, the right one, nails like little spades, rosy and moonless, cut practically short. There is a hand, a right hand, there moving into the line of my vision, preparing to knock, and there is nothing I can do to make it not, and there is nothing I want to do to make it not, and yet I think, *There is nothing I can do to stop this now.* I am going over the edge, plunging, my breath and my heart two feet above me and the rest falling.

***

I have seen pictures of them, pictures at weddings, at ball games, at home. I have heard their voices, Joe's uncannily like mine though he speaks a different dialect, has a different inflection, a different gender. I have written email to them both, I know the patterns of syntax they use both to say and write, the kinds of things that interest them. There before that door, then, I know so much about them, so much more than I know about most people I have never met before. Not to mention what my body knows, what knowledge that, because I am their daughter, I literally walk around in.

And yet. And yet. They are strangers to me, wholly unknown. I stand there with my fist raised, straining to hear their voices, to know what they are doing and thinking and saying there in that room waiting for this fist to come down, and I feel like a Jehovah's Witness must feel, before that first door at least but perhaps before them all, the series of doors that must be knocked on, must open, but may be shut, may shut quietly, may shut violently, but must be opened if anything is to happen.

And I stand there in front of that door with my fist raised and my heart pounding in my ears like the sea coming and going. And a little after nine on February 12, 1999, I set back my hand at the wrist like preparing a pendulum to swing, wind it up, and knock. Knock not knowing on what the door would open. Or even if it would, ever. Or even if I want it to.

***

My sister, of course, needed to know everything, every detail of those first minutes, every tiny minute shift of mood, every muscle turning under the skin, every pore opening and closing, everything. I couldn't tell her. I couldn't remember the details that way, I can't now. Meeting Anna and Joe is just a mass of impressions in my mind, not linear, not organized, nothing but a Seurat landscape. Dots here and there that give a general idea of things from a distance, that disintegrate up close.

What I remember is this.

I set my hand back on the wrist, I wind it up, I knock. I knock tentatively, I want them to have the option of not-hearing me knocking. But they must be waiting right there at the door, waiting for me to come and knock and to have to open the door. It unlatches to my right, gapes inward, brass hinges on my left; they glint in the motion of the door, in letting the light from the hall hit them. The door has a brass knob that shows me the motion of the door in little knowing winks, like the hinges do. The door is painted the color of the hall and blends in, almost camouflaged but for its moving. It opens to reveal other colors, like a wound before it bleeds has white around it and red inside.

There is a light on in the bathroom behind my mother. It catches in her hair, giving her an odd, fuzzy glory, a radiance like gilt in an old painting of the Madonna, pink and gold and lapis lazuli on wood. Behind her is white tile and a dark window, the chrome fixtures of the shower stall standing incongruously atop her right shoulder, to my left as she faces me. But she's not facing me, she's turned into the room a little, facing Joe. She is smaller than I am, considerably smaller, distinctly smaller. I feel like an oak in the presence of some delicate, pastel bloom that can't last longer than the time it takes to smell it, that browns under even the light heat of being touched. She wears glasses, her eyes owl-like behind them, her face is a triangle that comes to a point at her chin, wide at the temples. She wears a blue knit shirt, black knit leggings. Her toenails are painted red, the color of Christmas. She's holding a black shoe, peeling off with her free hand the price tag on its bottom.

She sees me, meets my eyes once, then shifts back to Joe, then says, "Hello." Then says, "Joe." Then moves out of the doorway to my right, handing the door to my father. To my father, who steps in to the open space she's left. He's big, solid. Looking at him, I feel right-sized, the size I ought to be—I've never felt like that, my whole life. Though he's tall and heavy, he never seems that way, just average, eye-level, on your level. He holds the door wide, filling the opening it makes, almost literally filling it, his arm an oblique angle at the elbow, the door pressing his right hip. He wears brown, medium brown pants, and brown shoes—deck shoes we used to call them. His shoulders are broad like mine. He looks at me like a starving person looks at food. I have seen pictures, I know they are brown eyes, but the color surprises me, it's not what I expected. The shade is different, and I remake my mind-image of them, standing there watching them watch me.

And he says, "Hello."

And I say, "Hello."

***

I am still in the hallway, my toes in my long black boots still inches from the seam in the carpet that separates their space from mine. Only when he steps back finally to the left into the place the door makes open, do I cross it, enter their room, and begin.

Impediments

The dark in October in Oakland, California, a quarter mile inland off the water, doesn't deter the night birds from coming in to walk on the sidewalks, to perch on the lamp-posts, to stare down from there at us two, standing, strange, beside the roadway. I rock foot to foot. He tucks his hands in his jeans pockets. We chat, just chat. The cold wind runs through his hair, then mine. I shiver, but I don't move closer, I can't be sure where that would lead. He is so tall that his voice passes above my head. The sea is somewhere in front of us. All day we have walked together. We end up on this corner, waiting. What for?

Literally, my nephew, the son of my birth-sister, who is taking me and my birthfather for dinner. My phone lights up: *Where are you?* I write: *Waiting.* My nephew writes: *Be there ASAP. Sorry.* I am shaking, the cold, my nerves, the shock of feeling awakened. The man beside me is searching for something to say to fill the silence. My nephew still does not appear.

Worry collects between my shoulder blades. I shift them, my dress moving against my back. I don't want to leave this corner, this man. My husband died three years ago. I have told this man that. ("That's not very long," he says.) The drip of time, him, the day, my dead husband whispering in my ear: *I told you to live. Live, just live.* But how?

Then comes this day, its clear sunlight, the smell of the sea and the brief sight of it at lunchtime, the faint warm scent of this man and of my own body in its clothes, the way the stoplight on this corner moves between its colors. The moment condenses to a single desire: take his hand, do not take his hand.

He says, to nothing and no one, but to me somehow: "Let me not to the marriage of true minds / Admit impediments." Here is a hook to hold onto. I concentrate on the poem, familiar from my education.

My face turns itself up to him: "That poem doesn't say what you think it does." Tense, wounded, nerdy. *Dumb, dumb, dumb,* I think, *why did I say that?* Immediately I want to die, actually to die. He stays silent, hands in his pockets, watching the traffic.

A seabird flutters out of the dark into the crosswalk and settles in a pool of streetlight, cars stopping and moving around it, it walking out of the way. I worry about the bird but nothing happens—the cars and the bird in some sort of dance. The next moment, my nephew waves at me from his truck.

I forget so much. This man, this Shakespeare, reminds me. (*I forget*, I say. *Remind me.*)

He asks why he has the poem wrong.

***

Let me not to the marriage of true minds
   Admit impediments.

It's on a chalkboard, the professor ex-military, a Marine who tells us he buzzes off his flattop when it's long enough for his wife to grab. We pretend not to understand that someone might grab his hair. We go, most nights, into our drunken selves, peeling down to skin and hair that we use for pleasure. This desire is not transferable to any professor, least of all this one. He is old, smiles tightly at us and barks sarcastically when we make mistakes. He has his back to us as he picks up a piece of chalk.

He writes: Let me NOT to the MARriage of TRUE MINDS.

He turns around. "Ictus," he says, "for stressed syllables. Mora for unstressed." I write this in my notes. I have no actual idea what he's talking about. I spell both *ictus* and *mora* wrong.

He writes the following on the board, each mark above a syllable, each syllable accounted for:

˘   ˘   ´   ˘   ˘   ´   ˘   ˘   ´   ´

Let   me   NOT   to   the   MAR   riage   of   TRUE   MINDS

I copy this into my notes, too. Still mystified.

He erases the words.

˘ ˘ ´ ˘ ˘ ´ ˘ ˘ ´ ´

He writes this on the board:

˘ ´ ˘ ´ ˘ ´ ˘ ´ ˘ ´ = iambic pentameter

He turns around, walks to the back of the room. A woman raises her hand. She says: "Sonnets are always in iambic pentameter." A statement of fact. I write it down, these words I've never heard before, fifty percent of that sentence a complete mystery. I don't dare ask. Everyone in the room is writing, or nodding, or both. I nod too.

Another person says: "That line is not iambic pentameter." The professor strides to the board then and dashes off another mystical set of illustrations:

This too, I copy. He says: "Anapest, anapest, anapest, ictus."
I stop taking notes, I am guessing at spelling, I am guessing everything.
A woman says, "Not pentameter."
Another woman says, "Not iambic."
The professor says, "Good. Why?"
There is silence. "Let's read the poem then," the professor says, and we do. Together, we do the standard reading: Love is not love that alters when things change, it's an ever-fixed mark, it persists through storms: this poem describes true, steady love. A love poem, a true love poem, a poem about immutable, true love.

I write this down. It's satisfying to know what the poem means. It's what, reading it last night, I thought it meant. It's satisfying to be right and to have everyone say what I think. The professor takes notes on the board. His hands are chalking up, the powder collecting in the vees between his fingers. He writes hard, quick little notes, underscoring words that mean "unchanging"; he circles the word *love* over and over again.

On the board across the way, next to the door, he writes the whole poem from memory:

> Let me not to the marriage of true minds
> Admit impediments. Love is not love
> That alters when it alteration finds
> Or bends with the remover to remove.

Oh no! It is an ever-fixéd mark
That looks on tempests and is never shaken;
it is the star to every wand'ring bark,
Whose worth's unknown though his height be taken.
Love's not Time's fool, though rosy lips and cheeks
Within his bending sickle's compass come;
Love alters not with his brief hours and weeks,
But bears it out even to the edge of doom.
If this be error and upon me prov'd,
I never writ, nor no man ever lov'd.
"It is dangerous," he says, "not to pay attention."

***

I'm fixing dinner when the phone rings. On the other end, Chuck says, "I love you so much," then, "I've been in an accident, can you come get me," then "I love you," again, then "I'm sorry." I shift immediately into doing, turning off the heat under the food, moving it to a cold burner, putting away the things that can't be left out, pushing the cat off the counter, saying into the phone: "Are you all right? Is everyone alright? Are you hurt? I'm coming, where are you?"

His voice is calm, it's never not calm. It's calm, but also slow and deliberate, like he's testing something, like he's working a theory through a miniscule hole. I get in the car and drive too quickly to the intersection a few miles from home where I find him, some police officers, and four or five clearly upset women and men standing beside a transfer truck loaded with huge spools of copper wire. The truck must weigh tons. On the verge sit three or four damaged cars, the worst is the one Chuck was driving whose hatchback is accordioned up nearly to the front seat. It's in a ditch off the shoulder, tilted slightly, looking like it knows it's not in the right place but can't remember how it got there.

Chuck looks at me, says, "I'm sorry, I'm sorry." Then, "I love you, sweetiepie," and "I'm okay, I'm really okay."

Me, I'm calculating, figuring the situation, trying to see just how close he was to dying. When it tallies, and I find I can't breathe, I sit down hard in the grass and concentrate on not throwing up. I am fighting with my own useless reaction: after all, he's fine, everyone is. He paces, his voice clipped and tense as he talks to the insurance agent on the phone. The police are writing a report, the driver of the truck standing by his open door wringing his hands and looking as if he's killed someone.

My husband walks back over to me and I hand him my water bottle. I discover then he's almost not capable of standing. This is not something he wants me to see, so he leans up against the wreck of the car and smiles, runs a hand over his head, adjusts his hair, drinks all my water at once. When the tow truck comes, we head home. It's nearly dark by then.

That night he is feverish in bed, if I move to get some space or roll over, his arm snakes out and racks me in again. He can't stand the simple separation of clothing, so peels it off himself and me and drops it to the floor. It's all skin, everywhere skin. He is calm, his hands calm on my skin, his voice in my ear as calm as quiet rain. Finally he falls asleep, almost dead asleep, so deeply I check his breathing. In the morning, in the shower, he tells me why no one died.

He had pulled up to the light and checked his rear-view mirror and had seen the transfer truck with its load of copper wire behind him. Only, he said, the thing wasn't braking. No nosing down, no sign that the driver was going to slow at all (at the accident site, it was clear the driver did not brake significantly before he hit Chuck's car).

In that few seconds—it could not have been more than that, really—my husband took his foot off the brake, shifted to neutral, and turned the wheel as hard as he could to the right. That way (he didn't think this, it was instinct) when the truck hit his car, it would move the straightline force of the collision to the right, his car absorbing some of the shock but flexing in it, moving it out of the way so that the truck barreling through would hit the line of cars in front of him with its momentum broken. Which is exactly what happened.

***

The form of a thing matters, my biology professor says. He plays clips from science fiction movies, showing us how stairs need knees, how windows indicate both eyes and eye-level, how flooring suggests feet.

The lights come up. In front of each pair of us he places an animal, long dead, its body pinned to black wax. Where there's no fur, its skin is raw looking. Its arms and legs are splayed to the four corners of the pan. Beside the pan are ten questions, none of them easy, none of them on the face of it asking for anatomy.

My dissection partner reads the first one.

"Name your animal for what is unique to it as an individual in its species. Find its idiosyncratic feature. Spend as much time as you need examining it. You may of course unpin it. You may delay the answer to this question until the end of your examination."

My lab partner and I, veterans of many such dissections ("Locate and draw your frog's heart" or "Find your pig's kidneys and remove them, placing them in a spare tray and labeling them left and right"), look at each other. He reads the second question.

"Your animal's mouth is designed for eating. What else is it designed for? Examine its mouth without using your scalpel and defend its purpose based on design."

Our animal is unfamiliar to us both. It is some sort of mammal, its fur wet, its eyes sunken. It has a long nose, and my lab partner gets out a tape measure, starts making notes. The nose ends in a narrowed point, nearly as narrow as the pad of my pinkie. We don't know what we're looking at, though we know the words for what we're observing. I write, *Long, narrow nose, flexible end, whiskers, eyes on either side of the head (prey?), underjaw narrow, significant underbite.* I pry open the mouth.

"Look," I say: "Canines, long and sharp, but all these molars, too. Omnivore." We write that down. The little pink tongue fills up the bottom jaw entirely. "But that's eating. What else could you do with this mouth?"

The nose is long, thin, tapered. I think: Rut. Stick it in places. I say, "I think this mouth is something it uses to find things—find things out in front of it, maybe for safety—is it a prey animal? Is that for running away from danger?"

We roll the animal over. Test its legs, think about its naked tail. My lab partner notes that its paws have different numbers of toes, but we don't know if this is normal for this species, so we just write it all down. Finally, we start in with our knives (Question 3: "Compare the animal's organs and their placement to your own and speculate about whether organ size or arrangement is foundational to the difference between you and your animal"). Which is when we discover we've got a marsupial.

I write this in the lab notes: *marsupial.* My lab partner measures and annotates a quick sketch with his numbers. We see if the nose fits into the pouch at all, but there's no way of telling, the spine so old and loose it could be: it could not be. The pouch itself is large and baggy, its lips lined with skin. The babies, none very big, would crawl in there to grow, a second uterus, an easier birth. I say, "Hey, bipeds could use this, yeah?" I write in our notes: *Marsupialism: better for us?* My lab partner looks over my shoulder, takes the pencil, circles this question. "Maybe," he says, "bipedalism is the gift we're always paying for." I say, "Maybe it's not a gift at all. All those stuck babies. All that lumbar compression."

"Makes you wonder," he says, "why anyone thinks God is in the details."

***

At the end of each line of the sonnet, the professor writes a letter.

Let me not to the marriage of true minds A
Admit impediments.   B

ABAB CDCD EFEF GG

"This," he says with his back to the room, his chalk pouncing on the board, "is part of why it's a Shakespearean or English sonnet." I write down the letters, the words *Shakespearean* and *English* next to the word *sonnet*. From the back of the room, a student coughs suddenly. The professor turns around, nods in this student's direction. It's one of the cool kids, an older student who sits in the back and says almost nothing. Now the student says, flatly and without rancor, "I think that's wrong."

The room freezes, palpably. The professor narrows his eyes and begins tossing chalk between his hands. There is chalk dust everywhere, both hands, up his arms, across his chest, the front of his khakis. I am waiting for the barking dismissal—inattention, rudeness, all kinds of infractions have meant students rushing from the room, sometimes crying, sometimes furious. But now just this silence and a kind of head-tipped listening.

The man in the back continues. "*Love* and *remove* don't rhyme. Neither do *come* and *doom*. *Lov'd* and *prov'd*." He coughs again, speaks even a little louder, "*Shaken* and *taken*. That's not right either." I turn around in my seat, the man with his back against the wall is looking at the ceiling. Several of us are staring at him, flicking our heads back and forth between him and the professor, waiting to see what happens next.

The professor backs up to the board and makes little tick marks next to the words that don't rhyme or there's something funny about. He says: "*Love* and *remove*, and *lov'd* and *prov'd*—eye-rhymes. *Come* and *doom* are off-rhymes. *Shaken* and *taken* are feminine rhymes, which just means their lines end in unstressed syllables." He makes marks for these on the board. "Those of you who can scan, which of these lines is iambic pentameter?" Three or four people take up the task. There is silence, the sound of pens working, then: "Which alters when it alteration finds?"—two students begin to argue about the word *when*. Stressed or unstressed? Iambic pentameter line or not? Another student says, "'Within his bending sickle's compass comes' is the only one." The professor nods and puts a tick mark by that line, and a question mark by the third line, the two students still pitching into each other about *when*. "Only one unarguably pentameter line in the whole thing," he says. "The question now is why."

I think: *why what?* No one says anything.

"Why," he says, "if a sonnet's pattern is supposed to be iambic pentameter, and if its subject is constant, regular, unchanging love, should there be all this"—he waves at the poem on the board—"this?"

More and more silence.

"And why," he says, "should it end in a conditional statement? And why," he's revving up somehow, to something I can't see and don't understand, "should you rhyme—or not, really—*love* with *remove*? Isn't that a joke? *Come* and *doom*?—and yes, it meant that then, too. When you do the scansion, what are all those unstressed syllables in the middle of those lines for? All that passivity, all that dropping off—the whole thing, it's just, it's just—" He trails off, circling bits of the poem, a period in the middle of the line right after *impediments*, the repeating *alter* and *remove*. It's like a puzzle, all the circles and lines, he's like a paranoid pasting pictures to a wall and stringing them together with a Sharpie and shoelaces looped on nails.

I don't dare ask what that means, but I'm writing it all down, tracing the same circles. I have no idea where any of this is leading.

But the man in the back does. He says, "Oh. Oh. The poem's a trick, isn't it? A riddle. The answer is: admit impediments all you can and will.

All the impediments. Look at them all." He's laughing now, actually laughing because he can see it. The professor is almost laughing now, too, as the man in the back coughs himself to silence, the puzzle solved for him. But not for me. I raise my hand, tentative, apologetically. I say, "I can see the puzzle"—*I can't*—"but I can't see how you got that." I am hoping that's enough for a walk-through. I am fixed in the professor's gaze.

"Emily," he says, "okay, so the poem seems to say one thing, but it doesn't say that at all if you pay attention, close attention. If you're looking at the details. The poet wants you to look, to notice that all that drivel about immutable love, the clichés, that's just poetry."

"So it doesn't say that love, real love, is immutable."

The man in the back, he's to my left, he's now so self-satisfied he almost purrs: "He means that whatever love is in a poem, it's not what you think it is. Like the whole sonnet thing, all those love poems, they aren't really. Sonnets about love. Though people think they are."

I address myself to the professor. "But how do you know?"

"Because the poem shows you that. You just have to look at it, how it's made, what it says because it's made that way. It's all impediments, no real rhythm, nothing but nice words capped with an if clause." Other students are catching on, you can hear them come awake to what's happening. One student says, "Can we do another one," as if poetry were crosswords or disappearing the Statue of Liberty.

"But," I say, "this is a poem too, why should we trust it, if it says not to trust poems? And what if that's—the scansion, the rhyme, that stuff—that's the true poem? Like, what you're saying is really love, like full of impediments and stuff, the opposite of that other stuff? Wait, what if—"

But from the other side of the room, another student, louder, cleverer, is talking over me, saying instead: "Do all the sonnets do this? Can we do that other one, you know the one with the summer's day in it?" The professor looks away, nods and opens his book, turns to the board. He erases all that work, all those impediments and all that love, replacing it with Sonnet 18, reading aloud as the words chalk themselves into lines we parse until the bell rings and releases us.

Leavings

His Dog's Knitted Shawl

I never knew that grief, the kind I'm in now, would be so like an injury to the body. I thought—when, to be honest, I thought about it at all—grief would feel "emotional." Your body not in the equation, just sadness, a feeling that one was lost or alone or bereft. How entirely wrong that is, how entirely incomplete. I was imagining a sandwich. Meager. Baloney and some bread. This is an Iowa farm, a harvest, a buffet, a harrow, a silo, miles of silos, mills, bake-houses, abattoirs and Ore-Ida factories. I was imagining the sniffles. This is end-stage rabies.

A long time ago now, a very long time ago now, a little beagle-mix puppy wandered out of the woods behind my house in Athens, Georgia. She had mange, she was starving, she was scared and dumb and young and all bones. I took her in. Named her Little Girl, because I had other, bigger male dogs and I didn't intend to keep her. But she got old with me. Snaggle-toothed and creaky. And when she got very old, so old she became doddering and feeble, she developed kidney disease and began wasting away.

Chuck and I started dressing her because as she wasted, she felt cold even in summer. She had a jaunty little jacket. She had a tee-shirt. Our favorite was a small, beige, knitted shawl that tied under her chin. She wore it like your grandma wore hers when she sat in a rocker shelling peas. Little Girl loved that shawl best, mouthing the fringe, wandering around shaking it into place now and then. Her lips never fitted over her teeth. We imagined she was smiling.

Kidney disease kills because you can't get clean. Metabolic toxins poison you. You become a trash-heap, a dump, you can't get rid of what is not-you, what is dead, what is killing you. In the end, at the very end, the pain and nausea are so intense there's no help but death. If death is actually peace and not just our moving pain to another place we can't visit.

A few days from her death, all Little Girl could do (in her knitted shawl) was pace, endlessly, for hours. Drink water. Vomit. Pace. Adjust her shawl. Pace. Vomit. Drink more water. Then she lay down in her shawl and, with our help, stopped breathing. Chuck cried for her, deeply, like a purgation. We kept the shawl because we had nothing else of her we could keep.

Yesterday, pacing, vomiting, trying to drink water, pacing, endlessly moving in circles through my house, through the yard, stopping to vomit in the grass behind a tree, trying to stop vomiting, pacing, I remembered Little Girl's dying. Same yard. Same thing. Walking, sometimes backwards, sometimes forwards, trying to walk away from the pain. When I wake up, my heart is flying around in the cage of my body, beating against my ribs and in my throat, my neck plugged into an electric socket and burning from the inside, my arms and legs herky-jerky and not to be depended upon, my torso a clenched fist around something sharp-edged like a corner, something biting, like bitter cold. I have morning sickness, hunched over the sink, vomiting bile. I have afternoon sickness, night sickness. Food poisons me. Air poisons me. I cannot get rid of the dead in my body.

My mind is unspeakable, but that's to be expected.

I never expected my body to try to become the corpse it's obsessed with.

My friends are concerned. They say: "Take the drugs." They say: "It will get better." They say—and I have asked this particularly—that there will be happiness, there will be something else later. They say: "It is time to be patient with yourself." They say: "You are stronger than you know."

But I am tired of strength. Chuck could move tree trunks. He is dead. Chuck fought off the flu in a day. He's dead. Chuck could go all day without eating. Chuck's dead. Chuck could hold me and let me cry, could bargain million-dollar contracts, control people he'd never met, pilot cars and boats, jackhammer driveways in one-hundred-degree heat, work eight hours without even noticing. He's dead. What is the use of strength?

This morning, at 5:26 am, I got up and began walking in circles in the house. Took care of the chickens just as the sun rose. Startled my mother, suffering from dementia, who was wandering around my bedroom calling my name. She wanted my phone number in case something happened to me. She wanted to give me hers so I could call her from wherever the dead go, with their phones. I lay down again. I shut my eyes. I dreamed the clock chimed three times and forgot the fourth note, distracted by its own ticking.

His Freckles

I know it's Chuck on the gurney. It's him. But when I get up close, I think it can't be him. It can't be him. The mouth is all wrong, a scrawl across his face, his chin tucked down tight to his neck, so tight the flesh spreads like a cowl below his earlobes. His hair is the wrong color, dark coppery brown, not the silver it was the last time I saw him, the beautiful run of silver down his back in that almost-metallic river. It's all wrong.

It's so wrong I can't believe it's him. I touch his head, cold as the room, solid, the right shape, it fits to my palm, I am taking his temperature, he has had the flu, I feel his hot head and say, "Oh sweetheart, you have a fever, stay in bed and I'll bring you something to drink." And he says, "There is something wrong with my back, shivers, I can't stop shivering." I say, "I'll get another blanket, it's the fever, it's fever." I put my hand on his hot, hot head. I am here and I can help and he will be well because I am here. *I am here, sweetheart, sleep while I watch you.*

The shape of his skull under my hand. I lift my hand, the foundation they've covered his face with coming away like a pale stain. It rubs off on his jacket where I hold him, so cold against my hands. I rub more off. I need to see his freckles, the scatter across his right temple, the dark one in front of his ear. I kiss them when they appear, crying away more foundation and more foundation, the brown spots finally how I know his body as his.

We are lying in bed, my head on his chest listening to his heartbeat. It's like the sound of the sea on the sand. It is a lullaby I understand, the sea in my blood, in my history. I am counting the freckles on his stomach, the constellation we named Umbilicus Major. There are seven planets, one like Jupiter, two small ones. The rest a cluster, an android belt scattered off to his left hip. I say, tracing each one with a finger, "You are the center of your own universe. Here you are orbited. Here is your gravitational field. Here you were born. Here worlds are born." His heart washes in and out. He laughs, moves a leg, kisses my forehead, my mouth, clicks off the light.

My engagement ring is an old diamond solitaire, bought in Amsterdam a hundred years ago, back when cutting didn't mean removing occlusions, back when occlusions identified a diamond. We take the stone and the mangled remains of its original setting to a local jeweler for reconstruction. Under the loupe, the tiny bit of unincorporated carbon looks enormous, like cracked pepper on a white tablecloth. The jeweler is delighted. Chuck is delighted. We will always know this diamond from any other. "Like us," Chuck says. "Unusual, us alone, no one else like us." We discover the same week that I have a deformed rib, it shows up in an x-ray like a squiggle in a cage of curves. Chuck falls asleep with his hand on it afterwards. "This is your tell," he says, "how I will always know you, how I will always find you no matter what happens. Like the carbon in your diamond."

There are no flaws, only points of identity. A broken pinkie finger, a damaged elbow, the scar on his nose that the puppy made, the flat back of my head, the broken veins on his knees. Like us, like us.

I take his dead hand, its nails with their half-moons of stale blood, cold as the room, cold as they got mid-winter in the night when he'd sneak them into my armpits, onto the back of my neck, between my legs. I chafe them, warm them against my face, for a second or two I can make it summer again, make them alive again, giving them my life, my warmth. And then it goes. I put my head on his chest, there is nothing. His sleeves are lined with plastic wrap. There are tiny plugs in his nose. They have stitched his eyes closed, the long lashes like the fringe on a lampshade. The light out. I kiss his dead mouth, a mouth I can't recognize, feel the teeth under his lips, recognizing those absolutely. My mouth, my face, is smeared with foundation. I can taste it.

The last thing he said, in person: "You have an owie. Do you want coverstick?" He held my face in his hands, looking through his glasses at the place, one thumb testing it. I rolled my eyes, backed out of his hands, got in the car, drove away. For a long time it didn't heal, a hard lump beside my mouth. Last week I discovered it had left a scar. I love this scar inordinately. It feels like the last mark he knew, like the dog-eared page of our lives together, like another way he'll know me, lost as I am, lost as he is. A friend wrote, *I've been watching* The Last of the Mohicans, *I think Chuck, Chuck, Chuck*. We used to mimic Daniel Day Lewis, *Stay alive, I will find you.* Stay alive, I will find you. You and only you. I will know you in your singular bones, Beloved, in your particular skin, in your very smell. If we meet again.

His Gladioli

It's all been a lie. It was a lie from the start. I am watching, now, the gardens die in front of me, as mine always did before I met him. I was never the gardener, really. Mine was a garden full of easy herbs. I'd chopped the soil with a mattock, I laid a small stone path. The whole thing was ten foot by ten foot, maybe. Sometimes things lived in it. Sometimes they didn't.

Before Chuck schooled me, what I knew about gardening I'd learned in my first marriage. Vegetables ("What is okra?" I asked my first husband), an old rose, some herbs. I liked to weed when things got very bad in my life. I would be writing my dissertation or ending my marriage, but really I would be pulling up unwanted growth by the roots, pennywort, chickweed, crabgrass. Pruning the one rose. Planting tulip bulbs that drowned in too much shade and never bloomed.

When I met Chuck in Wisconsin, I told him I killed plants. To trust nothing to me. This was a truth.

He moved in and everything changed, everything greened up. We'd bundle into our coats, set out in April, in May, looking for that first shoot of green somewhere we'd planted. He rescued our lilacs, he built a pond, constructed two berms. Solved a drainage issue, saved our street's horse chestnuts simply by insisting to the city government that they not be cut down. Every June, we would watch the older woman across the way set out her eight red geraniums, evenly spaced against her foundation. We would say to ourselves: this is not us. We are not the red geranium crowd. Then we would make more compost, spread more manure, plant grapes and a Jane magnolia and bridal-veil spirea and a huge wall of forsythia. Everything we planted would live, luxuriate, grow so tall and so fast we could scarcely credit it.

When we bought the house in Georgia with its nearly two acres of pine forest and lawn, he began digging, planning, planting. One day he said, as nearly defeated as I ever saw him, "This is too much land. I don't know how to organize it." He never stopped trying, not after the first twenty-four square feet of vegetable garden dug in, improved, improved again. Not after the next six plots the same size as that, the garden that wound across the front of the house like a thick snake, not after building rock retention walls to keep the new rich dirt where he wanted it. He started a miniature vineyard and planted six Concord vines, then three more, then a dozen that fruited some seventy pounds of grapes the year he died. Up near the road he built out a small wildlife habitat full of perennials bought half-price at the local garden store. He set out a Bartlett pear (with a partridge) I bought him for our anniversary and waited for the fruit. His small orchard included cherry trees, apple trees, an apricot, a peach tree, an almond. He loved Japanese maples and put in four or five of these. We planted heritage roses, Cordelia, Caldwell's Pink, Blossomtime, Vineyard Song, Fortuniana, Lady Banks, the unnamed chinas. He built rock borders, rock paths, a sprinkler system he hand-designed. Gardenias, azaleas, hydrangeas, daylilies. Trumpet vines. Blueberries, blackberries, raspberries. Endless self-replicating irises and daisies and purple coneflower.

Three years before he died, he bought half a dozen salmon-red gladiola bulbs, put them in a corner of the rose garden. They didn't come up. They were dead, we thought. But the next year? Magic. A dozen spires. When he died, nearly two dozen were spiking out of the ground. They bloomed a few weeks later, rolling out their red, cupped flags in a sort of insistent grouping. Even the aphids were impressed. His gladioli, brave, red, resilient, compiling themselves underground when they looked fast asleep or dead.

They were not his favorite plants. He loved best what doesn't grow in Georgia's hot climate, though he insisted on replanting and replanting them when they withered. Delphinium was his favorite of favorites, the blue the color of the sky above the Chesapeake where he grew up, their form a cone of loveliness he remembered in his grandmother's gardens, there in front of the twelve-foot-tall hollyhocks in their foamy pink and white, and in front of both, mounds of something, he never told me what, but he drew it in my mind as we lay in the hammock or on the grass watching the sky turn itself over into night. "Green," he'd say, "mounds of green like chrysanthemums, only not them at all." His arm under my head fit perfectly. The grass, the night, smelled of crushed good things, food and health. The dog shook his head and rolled beside us.

He said, "My grandmother had a square stone bird bath. It stood in front of a tree and the mourning doves sat in the shade when it was hot." And then he would coo just like a dove into the dusk and somewhere, sleepily, a dove would answer. He'd laugh then, roll over into my side, kiss my face, my ear, my hair. The grass, the hammock, the world would be set in motion then, and he would pull me to my feet, the stars spinning out now over us, lighting their own special pinholes in the universe. And we would go inside, the names of our plants incantations on our tongues. Sweet almond, balloon-flower, bleeding heart, dianthus. Outside our windows, the whole green world was building itself, and we ate dinner and went to bed in love with the morning to come that had such beauty in it.

The year he died, his gladioli glowed all day in the light like strings of Christmas bulbs. They come from little brown nubs of nothing, set right under the soil. He is dead. They go on, though he can neither see nor sense them, though he is dead and doesn't go on at all. How is that possible, really, his gladioli without him? How are they blooming? How does anything bloom without him, the gardenias, the daisies, the coneflowers in his garden, the bee balm and the roses?

Sweetheart, with your hands in the dirt, and your face lit with the sun, are you in a garden somewhere, one that's in sight of your bay, in sight of your grandmother's house crammed full of everything old and broken and comfortable, just as she liked it? Do the hollyhocks dwarf her, are the delphinium the exact color of her eyes, or the sky, or both maybe, so beautiful she was and how you loved her? And are you saying to her, *What a magnificent garden, Grandma, so full of everything and what are those plants, and what are those*, and is she saying, *Come sit with your grandfather and me and bring your coffee, and let's talk*? Are there dogs milling there, and your cats, Chessie and Lo-kai and Fauna and Gracie young again, winding into the greenness? Sometimes, in the breeze, does your hair lift off your neck and do you think of the garden you left with me, the grapes rounding out and beetle-chewed, the way the weeds choke everything? And do you think of me sometimes, crying in your garden for you? Are you waiting, are you there, are there gardens where you are?

When the wind comes, his gladioli bend over and fall, their flowers sticking in the red clay.

His Hours

Six weeks after he dies, I have to find a paperclip. This means opening the permanently closed door to his office, the place he worked from every day, hours and hours on end. Sometimes seventy hours a week.

The last time I saw him, in his tee-shirt from Apalachicola and the green canvas carpenter pants I bought him for Christmas, he was just ending a call with a group of CIOs from Texas. All the big, powerful men who somehow (of course, I thought) listened to Chuck when he described what to do, how to fix things, how to make things work. He said: "I have just told the CIOs what to do. Me." He pretended to be humbled. I said: "Will they do it?" He said: "Of course. I told them. It's right."

He walked me to the foyer and we stood in the light coming through the front door. He looked at my face, held it in both hands, his thumbs on both sides of my mouth. He kissed and kissed me. I did not want to leave, I did not want to leave him or the dogs or the house. Him. I was going to give a big talk in Indiana. It was an honor, I could not have turned it down. But I never wanted to leave, never wanted to go away, no matter for what. I never felt I would find my way home. No adopted person ever thinks they're coming back. I said: "I don't want to go." He said, "But you will and you'll be home the day after tomorrow and tell me all about how they loved your talk." He held me, looked at me, loved me. Backing down the driveway, I saw him through the kitchen window washing his hands, the way his shoulders moved against his tee-shirt, the way his back curved, the way his hair traced the cleft of his spine between his shoulder blades.

When I got home, that shirt, those pants, were on the bed. I triple-wrapped the shirt so I could smell him, later. I threw out the pants.

When I go into his office to get the paperclip, I find instead a drawer full of notepads tracking his work hours, two full years of work, hour by hour. He saved them all. So much time, so much work. I lifted them out of the drawer and spread them on the floor. I sat down among them and watched the windows darken, the way the leaves on the holly just outside sifted shadows and light through the windows in elongating patterns. The notebooks all around me, so many pages. So much time.

In that dark room, so dark eventually I can see nothing at all, not even my hand touching the pages, I lift one and blow on it. I watch the hours dissolving with my breath into actual time, the ticking of the grandfather clock in the hall, backwards, until Chuck is sitting again in this dark, and I come and say to him: "You will die. Get up, come with me, let's go to bed, hold hands, hold each other. Hold my face in your hands and see me, let me put you to sleep combing your hair with my fingers. Touch me. Talk to me. Say my name again and again, and let us wake up at dawn together."

These hours, this one page, just these. (He doesn't have a paperclip anywhere.)

His Love Note

I never read his journals, not while he was alive. There were so many of them, most of them from his much-younger days. One he kept of our lives, but not regularly. Sometimes. When he had time. He didn't have time very often.

On a day after a drive, my mother in her dementia beside me reading road-signs out loud and asking: "Why are there trees, why so many trees?" I missed his mind like a ferocity. I missed the way he saw things, described things, what he noticed, what he knew.

So I read his journal. First, the blue notebook full of loathing for his work, frustration with where we lived, filled with dark, swampy anger. Then the hardbound volume I bought him many years ago, early in the relationship. On the first unlined page I had written, "Just write." He had razored out that page, many pages. The spine furred up like a Mohawk when I opened the cover. But in the front, a clutter of things: pictures of where he'd grown up, newspaper clippings, email and notes about his grandparents' deaths. And the letter I'd written him after our first anniversary, now decades ago:

"What to wear? The perennial first-date question. I consulted Chitra, the only one besides John who knew I was going to see you that night. 'Blue,' she said, 'and a short skirt.' Then, 'No, red or orange. Not blue.' And so I went home, put on clothes that were blue, a short skirt, took them off, put on black, took it off, then decided: salmon sweatshirt and black tight pants. Black shoes. No make-up so no false promises, have me or not as I am, as I was. And so I went, thinking I could not remember your face, only knew this disembodied voice, velvet cat-tongued, rough as a purr, hours and hours of it, and that instant sweat in Savannah. I wanted so much just to taste you, I wanted even as I drove there, to set my teeth into, against you, as one does a firm, tart fruit. I didn't love you then.

The wind set me on edge, whipping and whipping the trees nearly to the ground when I wended my way there—your anxious voice not two blocks away on my phone, 'Where are you? Are you still coming?'—and then I pulled into the hospital driveway, debating: 'Motor off? Motor on? In the car? Out?' I decided I wanted to see you first, before you saw me, to have that advantage, and so I got out of the car. Stood on the running board, peered through all that glass. I was so afraid I wouldn't know you to see you, then talked myself out of it, remembering your hair—how many men, I told myself, have such ponytails? and work here?—And thus calmed, I set myself to braiding mine, restraining it, so pushed into a frenzy by the incessant wind—and turned profile to the glass, face to the wind instead for one moment. In that moment, you were there and said something like, 'Wow, you're gorgeous'—making me blush in frustration, looking down, elsewhere, away—not having seen first.

And so you drove, we walked, ate, kissing in the wind blowing our hair now, almost inseparable into our two mouths meeting. I don't know when I began to love you, only that I knew I would—does this count?—the next day, opening your email, reading all crammed into one line the same joy I had felt, had feared finding all alone, not-shared joy. And I knew that I had loved you for some time when waking one night—which, I don't know—I watched you sleeping, your hair tumbled and nearly alive, your one leg warm over mine, your breath like the breezes off the sea, humid and home. And so I came to love you after this night two months ago now—after days and nights full of you and us, talking and touching and laughing and everything people do together when they love—

I have nothing to give you tonight but this, no coral, no notebook, no solid something that represents the thing more valued and less tangible:

Here instead is my time, my thoughts, my mind, my spirit, my attention, my heart, my life, my love. Will it do?"

He saved this letter—I wrote him often in those days, ink on paper, any paper I could find. He saved this one.

I want to have kept his first letter to me, illegible, labored over for hours, ludicrously short. It said something like, "Thanks for the cookies, they were great, email me [address]." I don't know that I did. I thought I would have him forever. What did I need that note for?

He came to me in a dream some months after he died. He called my name twice in a way I'd never heard him do, so much yearning. Typescript appeared in front of my eyes, my name, twice. The pain in my chest broke like the top of a cake. I said, *The dogs are safe, the cats are safe, the chickens are safe.* I am not safe, though. I will never be safe again.

I said: *Sweetheart, I can hear you.* I said: *If you are testing the system, I can hear you. Say more, say more, say anything. I can hear you.* I said: *Tell me where you are? Write down your address. I will write you every day, I will mail what I write to you, I will read it aloud in my dreams to you. Here, give me your hand, your pen, that slip of paper, write where you are to me and I will put a pin in it on a map, I will pin this slip of paper to it, and every trip to the mailbox there you will find me, my heart, my life, my love. An address. Where are you?*

I woke up. Last night, I dreamt only that I was walking in the green woods, the gray stems of the trees like striations of light, towards a cabin made of new yellow wood, empty and with a long, steep staircase to the roof. Chuck wasn't there, though I looked everywhere for him.

His Son

It is Tuesday, April 14, 2015. We hang up the phone, me on one extension, him on another. Chuck shoots out of his office like he's been slung around the sun in some *Star Trek* episode in which time runs backwards. He dances. He sings. The words to the song are something like "Papa, papa, daddy daddy daddy." He grabs me, lifts me off the ground, swings me in a full circle. My ankle bangs something hard. The day he dies, I finger the bruise until I rub the spot raw. He sets me down, then dances his version of the mashed potato, only with herky-jerky leg action. He giggles, his voice two octaves too high. He grabs my left arm and my right and dances me into the center of the room, where he kisses me like he cannot kiss me enough. He says: "You are going to be a mama. We are going to be parents. Us. Us."

Fourteen years before, we lost the first one. Then another one. Then another.

Six years before, another, five years before, another one. Washed away, taken away, never really there. But this is different. This one is real. This one is going to be a son. We can have him, keep him. He will be ours, in our life together. Chuck looks at me, his eyes behind his glasses all pupil in the half-dark room. He says: "Everything will be new. A whole new life. For us. For us. All changed. All different and new."

I say, "Is that okay?"

He looks thoughtful. "Of course," he says. "Of course. Our son is coming. Can you believe it?"

I pace while he gets dinner together, just bowls of things, olives, fruit, cheese. His packaged apple pie. I pace, trying out *mother*, trying out—oh my god oh my god—our *son*. We get into bed, take the tray of food with us. He is quiet for a while. Then he says: "Will I be a good father?" I push the tray away, shove my face into his neck, breathe in, breathe out. He smells delicious, like home, like my own skin. I say: "Oh Jesus, sweetheart, the very best ever. Your son will love you better than everything in the world. You cannot imagine the good you will be. I'll be Safety Mom and you'll be Fun Daddy and our son will be loved to the skies and know it. You cannot imagine." He takes my hand, kisses me. He says, "I will do the best I can." I say, "I cannot imagine your doing otherwise, when have you ever done otherwise, Love?" He rubs my thumb with his. He says, "We should decide on a name." I say, "Easy. Caldwell. I love your middle name. We could call him Cal. You know, like, 'Cal, cut that shit out,' and, 'Cal, no playing in the litter box.'"

"Cal," he says. "That's good. Then Victor as a middle name, for my grandfather?"

"Yes," I say. "Victor."

He says, "Nothing from your family?"

I say, "We can add my last name if you want, but I don't care. I'll know he's my boy. He'll know he's mine. Caldwell Victor Bowie."

He goes silent. "That's a great name," he says.

Our son.

He kisses me, rolls over, goes to sleep.

It is Tuesday night. Friday morning, Chuck is dead. The world stops, or goes on, or both, hideously.

Six weeks later, I lose our son like I lost Chuck, like I lost all our life together. Not to death but to the law that stipulates he needs a father. And a lawyer, and another thirty-to seventy-thousand dollars and maybe two or three years through the courts, with no assurance that I can keep the child, since his birthfather is refusing to relinquish him. I say, "I'm adopted, I cannot endure this, I could not force a birthfather to relinquish his son, I could not live in the knowledge I might have to let him go, too, if I can't force his birthfather to give up." I say: "This is just impossible. This is not possible." The last phone call I have with the facilitator is a hodgepodge of maybes, you coulds, if you justs. I say goodbye and never speak of this again to anyone.

And so our son spills out of my hands like cinders, like stones, everything bruised already, now scraped hard and bloodied. His son, never his son, him never a father, us never parents. I ask Chuck in my sleep, in my waking, how much more can we lose together, being apart? I want him to come back to me, to unspool the time in a great smooth unrolling, a satin ribbon of time with our whole lives on it. I want to find the place where we are together again, I want him to give me back himself, our lives, our son. Why not? I saw him do so many impossible things. Why not this, too?

THE AUTHOR

Emily Hipchen is a Fulbright scholar, the editor of *Adoption & Culture*, co-editor of the book series *Formations: Adoption, Kinship, and Culture* (OSUP), and an emeritus editor of *a/b: Auto/Biography Studies*. She's an editor of *Inhabiting* La Patria*: Identity, Agency, and* Antojo *in the Works of Julia Alvarez* (SUNY 2013) and of *The Routledge Auto|Biography Studies Reader* (2015). She has edited *The Routledge Critical Adoption Studies Reader* (2023) and is co-editor of *The Routledge Companion to Auto/Biography Studies* (forthcoming, 2027) as well as six journal special issues. She is also the author of a memoir, *Coming Apart Together: Fragments from an Adoption* (2005), and of the scholarly monograph *Frankenstein's Kinjob: Adoptive Life* (forthcoming, OSUP, 2027). Her essays, short stories, and poems have won multiple awards and have appeared in *Fourth Genre, AGNI, Cincinnati Review*, and elsewhere. She directs the Nonfiction Writing Program at Brown University, where she teaches nonfiction.